book to be returned on or before
below or you will b

in poetry and prose

LONDON

in poetry and prose

Compiled by

Anna Adams

Drawings by

Neil Pittaway

London
ENITHARMON PRESS
2003

First published in 2003
by the Enitharmon Press
26B Caversham Road
London NW5 2DU

www.enitharmon.co.uk

Distributed in the UK
by Central Books
99 Wallis Road
London E9 5LN

ISBN 1 900564 03 3

British Library Cataloguing-in-Publication Data.
A catalogue record for this book is available
from the British Library.

Typeset in Bembo by Servis Filmsetting Ltd
and printed in England by
Antony Rowe Ltd

CONTENTS

8

FOREWORD

Noisy, stimulating, deadening, filthy, mysterious, tolerant, racist, crime-ridden, saint-haunted, ancient, up-to-the-minute, oppressive, liberating, crowded, lonely, addictive, and green-and-gardened, London is a microcosm of the World. Most cities are, and poets need cities as well as solitude, for, besides publishers, bookshops, conversation and appreciation, poets need a random selection of humanity, including other poets. City hubbub may well drown the still small voice of the muse for a while, but this durable spirit should get its breath back once it is acclimatised, or else carry home to its native heath or valley much interesting grist for the poetic mill.

Even wild Wordsworth lived in London for a spell, and the shy Clare came visiting three times. Perhaps he should have come more often; he might have been less lonely and less mad. While in London he met poets, saw plays and observed Londoners: and he was not always intimidated by them. Even Hazlitt did not frighten him unduly, and Cary, the translator of Dante, was extremely kind to him. His fellow 'peasant', Thomas Hardy, left Dorset and lived for several years at Westbourne Park Villas, though he carried his internalised Wessex with him wherever he went. Ted Hughes, that Northerner who took refuge in Devon, came (after Cambridge) to seek his fortune in London. The American, T. S. Eliot, made London his home. He saw it as old and sordid but wrote about it in a new way, as though all time were simultaneous. His lines are haunted by Dante, Webster, Spenser and Shakespeare, yet they remain new. Chaucer was a native-born Londoner who learned Italian as a child in Lombard Street. He then travelled abroad, learned his art from Boccaccio the Florentine, and brought his poetic skills home to London where he wrote *The Canterbury Tales*. Samuel Johnson was a provincial, from Lichfield, who became a typical Londoner. But the truest and most unlikely one was the unworldly William Blake. He was born near Golden Square, in Soho, and he never went north of Barnet or south of Felpham, near the Sussex coast; and he only went there once, but stayed three years. Then he and his wife returned thankfully to their native city.

William and Kate Blake were pieces of London: born and bred in the metropolis, or as near as makes no matter, so every poem that William wrote, though it might be about some mythical kingdom, could be regarded as a voice of London. One of the voices: for Keats was born in Finsbury. Though Enfield and Edmonton, where he spent much of his childhood, were not part of London then, they are now, and so is Battersea where Kate Blake's father kept a market-garden; and Hampstead, where Keats wrote his 'Ode to a Nightingale', is nowadays as much a part of London as is Hammersmith or the Isle of Dogs. So I have claimed Keats's 'Nightingale' as a London poem; and Keats's Fairyland, where 'The Cap and Bells' is set, is really London, and Shelley's 'Hell', MacNeice's 'Laredo' and Blake's 'Jerusalem' are London too.

The advantage of capital cities is that they are not usually engaged in primary production, but live on the surplus created by farming, fishing, forestry and mining that makes civilisation possible. As well as trade, they are involved in the arts, and the evaluation and interpretation of art. A capital city should be the great ideas-exchange of a country, though it may exchange so many commodities that it can become a noisy knot of confused fashions rather than truths. Nevertheless poets need these places, and many poets are entirely urban, as Blake was. But in his day London was smaller. It was small enough for him to walk right out of it and find – somewhere – that beautiful flower of chalky downlands, the Pasque Flower that adorns the title-page of his first prophetic book, *The Book of Thel*.

So Blake should not be thought of as being hemmed in by streets, though he lived in several: Green Street, Broad Street, Poland Street, South Molton Street and Fountains Court; and he would have walked along most of the old throughfares that survive today. Yet his London was not our London. He saw it as a fallen, suffering and materialised Jerusalem, a travesty of the heavenly city that he thought humanity ought to inhabit.

It would obviously be impossible to include the whole of Blake's great psychodrama – however many street-names it may contain – in this small anthology, so I have contented myself with extracts, and with using a few of Blake's mighty lines as epigraphs for each of my twelve sections. I hope that by using Jerusalem in this way I don't seem to belittle it; I intend, by tantalising people with fragments, to lead them to read the whole of Blake's hundred pages. Also, I like to think that the extracts and fragments will wander through my book's pages like glimpses of the spirits of young William and Kate, as Los and Enitharmon, going for their day-long, thirty-mile walks round the environs of the city which has, in two hundred years, spread like a splash of spilt coffee over the map of the Thames basin.

In their day Green Lanes were green, Wood Green was wooded, Herne Hill may have had a heronry, Camberwell was a village that gave its name to a butterfly, Primrose Hill and St John's Wood must have contained both primroses and woods, and Old Oak Common Lane was a truthful description of the road it named.

In those days the North Circular Road and the M25 were horrors undreamed of, as were the skeins of metal railway tracks and the huge, sooty mainline stations north of the Marylebone Road, which we have begun to feel both fond and proud of since we have cleaned them up. Marylebone was once an area of pleasure-gardens. Saint Mary by the Bourne was the church of the Manor of Tyburn, named after the boundary brook that flowed through North-west London. The name of Tyburn today makes us remember the gallows that stood where 'mournful, ever-weeping Oxford Street', along which condemned felons passed to execution, met the Edgware Road. Somers Town, where Blake's contemporary, Mary Wollstonecraft, went to live as a single parent with her little daughter Fanny, was a village outside London, and the Lambeth where William Blake saw his vision of a world in a grain of sand still had much that was rural about it. There William and Kate lived in Hercules Buildings where, he said, he had 'a whole house to roam in'. There was also a garden, with a grapevine that was trained and pruned by Kate, the gardener's daughter; and the young couple used to play at Adam and Eve there.

Years later William wrote:

There is a Grain of Sand in Lambeth that Satan cannot find
Nor can his Watch Fiends find it: 'tis translucent and has many
    Angles
But he who finds it will find Oothoon's palace; for within
Opening into Beulah every Angle is a lovely heaven.

Blake saw eternity in everything and understood that the imagination was the true reality. He saw Londoners deluded by materalism, as they still are today. He saw

London, blind and age-bent, begging through the streets
Of Babylon, led by a child;
. . .
The corner of Broad Street weeps; Poland Street languishes:
To Great Queen Street and Lincoln's Inn all is distress and woe.
The night falls thick . . .

Indeed it did, for the Industrial Revolution was upon us.

In my youth too the night fell thick, but for a different reason: the Second World War, with blackout and – from time to time – storms of bombs. Today it seems like a dream to remember the sirens, the imperturbable barrage balloons, the searchlights, throbbing skies, clatter of anti-aircraft fire, the showers of shrapnel striking sparks from paving-stones, and the surreal dormitory Underground. There are half a dozen, at least, air-raid poems of Louis MacNeice that I would have liked to use in the 'Recent Wars' section, for he weathered out the six years in London, and had the courage and presence of mind to write about it while it was still going on.

I, as a teenage art student, used to spend some of my leisure exploring, with a friend, the latest bomb damage of 1943 and 1944. We looked at the exposed interiors, the broken walls and rubblescapes. One weekend, Whitfield Street, in Bloomsbury, was still standing, and the next weekend most of it had been blown away. One evening there was a crowded pub on a street-corner, and a few days later there was a scattered ruin and the bare trees of a nearby square were hung with tatters. One day we slipped through a broken side door into a palatial space of red plush couches, curving staircases with gilded bannisters, shattered mirrors, deep pile carpets strewn with fallen plaster and dust, pieces of chandeliers and other remainders of ruined opulence. We were completely mystified and slightly awestruck by it. What could it have been? We had never in our lives set foot in such a place. 'Was it a high-class brothel?' we wondered naively, for the place had a sinful air. Looking back, I suspect it of having been one of the better Lyons Corner Houses.

We did a certain amount of drawing of what we saw, and I have often wished that I had made more of my sketches of eviscerated dwellings with dangling plumbing, torn wallpapers and broken stairs on view. But grown-up artists – Minton and Sutherland and John Piper – were doing it for us, fortunately, while Louis MacNeice, Stephen Spender and others wrote about the bombers and the bombed.

MacNeice thought of the planes prowling in the night skies above us, not as 'the Jerries' but as 'trolls' –

In the misty night humming to themselves like morons
They ramble and rumble over the rooftops, stumble and shamble
    from pile to pillar,
In clodhopping boots that crunch the stars
And a blank smirk on their faces:
    Pretty Polly won't die yet.

12

He understood that the enemy was not a particular nationality or breed of men but the will to mindless destruction, and the hate that skulks in all of us.

It was, of course, wonderful when streetlights were allowed to shine again, and shop windows were unboarded and displays of goods lit up; but the sober, non-commercial, neon-free London had its own beauty, and because those war years were our formative years we had grown up with an ingrained taste for austerity. I still remember the naturally moonlit nights, and the pitch-dark overcast and starless nights when you could only tell the difference between soldiers and civilians passing along the pavement by the clump of army boots and the chemical smell of uniforms. I remember seeing winter sunsets from beside the lake in Regent's Park, with distant buildings as blue as far off mountains, and the descending sun a luminous pink disc in the misty sky. I remember London University from Gower Street as a huge cliff, or iceberg, white in the moonlight that cast sharp-edged shadows across traffic-free streets. And in Summer there was waist-high grass in the London squares, for there was no labour to spare for mowing lawns. As often as not this luxuriant growth hid romping lovers, for many people got through the war under an erotic anaesthetic. So moon and star light, long grass, lovers, and flocks of sheep grazing in Hyde Park, gave wartime London a Palmeresque aspect not fully appreciated at the time.

After 1945, when two Japanese cities were destroyed by two of the Allies' atom bombs, a perception grew in the hearts of many people that cities were not places of safety but rather places of greatest danger. A not entirely irrational romantic impulse took root and grew in our semi-conscious minds. We longed to get away to the wild innocent places, and, by the time I was thirty, I and my mate, with two small children, decamped from London and stayed away for thirty years. I don't regret this, for I was re-educated at the university of Upper Ribblesdale, in Yorkshire, where I experienced a great deal of solitude and was able to hear myself think. And I read, and began to write seriously, putting the pressure on. And I learned a new environment.

In that hard though beautiful landscape I learned how much work goes into producing that surplus of essentials that maintains cities. I learned that nature may be beautiful but it is not benevolent, and though country people can sometimes seem hard, wild nature is harder. We had chosen, or chanced upon, a fairly exposed and non-cooperative country to lead our lives in; but there I also learned that

13

in a cold climate humans are warmer to one another. Finally, I was convinced that there is no place of safety from mankind's engines of destruction, for the world is one world.

By the time our children were grown up we had begun to detect an impulse in ourselves to return to the city: so when an opportunity offered itself, we took it, and I found myself living in the heart of London, or, to be more exact, in the upper attics of Burlington House which comprise the 'Keeper's Studio'. So I shopped in Soho and we took sundry morning walks in St James's Park. How exhilarating it was for those first few years! How various is the city! How tolerant and cosmopolitan! How oppressive and how free! But how noisy and how smelly! How unfair and how bad-mannered! And how expensive!

But it was, after all, our home town, and we loved it.

This anthology is meant to celebrate it. 'But why only in verse?' I began to wonder half way through. John Clare wrote no poetry about London, but it drove him to quite a lot of his punctuation-free prose. So he was welcomed in. Then I lacked a good thick pea-souper fog for my weather section, and I remembered the opening of Dickens' *Bleak House*. Once that author had his foot in the door I could not keep out his eloquent anger on the subject of London's poor and neglected children. Then Thomas de Quincey, I recollected, had once been down-and-out in London. He had referred to Oxford Street as his 'stony-hearted stepmother', for he knew what it was to lie in shop-doorways. So I invited him in, holding his lost friend Ann by the hand. Then Dr Johnson, pontificating, was led in by Boswell. And so on, until we became quite a crowd.

Many London poems, from Chaucer onward, tend to be comic. 'The Fortunes of War', by Kit Wright, is comic with tragic undertones, as is 'The Stations of King's Cross' by D. J. Enright. 'How Pleasant it is to have Money' is underlaid by the thought of how unpleasant it is not to. Cities necessitate a sense of humour; it is one of the means of surviving them. So a plentiful variety has winged in to roost among my categories, and I don't think of any genre as higher or lower, for, as Blake said: 'In the Kingdom of Poetry, all are equal.' If they are true poems, however slight, they can keep company with one another.

And he also said, 'Enough, or too much.'

ANNA ADAMS

1

THE GREAT WEN

I behold London, a Human awful wonder of God.

William Blake, *Jerusalem*

WILLIAM WORDSWORTH
(1770–1850)

Rise Up, Thou Monstrous Ant-hill on the Plain

Rise up, thou monstrous ant-hill on the plain
Of a too busy world! Before me flow,
Thou endless stream of men and moving things!
Thy every-day appearance, as it strikes –
With wonder heightened, or sublimed by awe –
On strangers, of all ages; the quick dance
Of colours, lights, and forms; the deafening din;
The comers and the goers face to face,
Face after face; the string of dazzling wares,
Shop after shop, with symbols, blazoned names,
And all the tradesman's honours overhead:
Here, fronts of houses, like a title-page
With letters huge inscribed from top to toe;
Stationed above the door, like guardian saints,
There, allegoric shapes, female or male,
Or physiognomies of real men,
Land-warriors, kings, or admirals of the sea,
Boyle, Shakespeare, Newton, or the attractive head
Of some quack-doctor, famous in his day.

Meanwhile the roar continues, till at length,
Escaped as from an enemy, we turn
Abruptly into some sequestered nook,
Still as a sheltered place when winds blow loud!
At leisure, thence, through tracts of thin resort,
And sights and sounds that come at intervals,
We take our way. A raree-show is here,
With children gathered round; another street
Presents a company of dancing dogs,
Or dromedary, with an antic pair
Of monkeys on his back; a minstrel band
Of Savoyards; or, single and alone,
An English ballad-singer. Private courts,
Gloomy as coffins, and unsightly lanes

Thrilled by some female vendor's scream, belike
The very shrillest of all London cries,
May then entangle our impatient steps;
Conducted through those labyrinths, unawares,
To privileged regions and inviolate,
Where from their airy lodges studious lawyers
Look out on waters, walks, and gardens green.

FELIX MENDELSSOHN
(1810–47)

It is fearful! It is mad!

It is fearful! It is mad! I am quite giddy and confused. London is the grandest and most complicated monster on the face of the earth. How can I compress into one letter what I have experienced in the last three days! I hardly remember the chief events, and yet I dare not keep a diary, for then I should have to see less of life, and that I do not wish. On the contrary, I wish to take everything that offers itself. Things toss and whirl about me as if I were in a vortex, and I am whirled along with them. Not in the last six months in Berlin have I seen so many contrasts and such variety as in these three days. Just turn to the right from my lodging, walk down Regent Street and see the wide, bright thoroughfare with its arcades (alas! it is again enveloped in a thick fog today) and the shops with signs as big as a man, and the stage-coaches piled up with people, and a row of vehicles left behind by the pedestrians because in one place the smart carriages have crowded the way! See how a horse rears before a house because his rider has acquaintances there, and how men are used for carrying advertisements on which the graceful achievements of accomplished cats are promised, and the beggars, and the negroes, and those fat John Bulls with their slender, beautiful daughters hanging on their arms. Ah, those daughters! However, do not be alarmed, there is no danger in that quarter, neither in Hyde Park, so rich in ladies, where I drove about yesterday in a fashionable manner with Mme. Moscheles, nor at the concerts, nor at the Opera, (for I have already been to all those places); only at the corners and crossings is there any danger, and there I sometimes say softly to myself, in a well-known voice: 'Take care lest you get run over'. Such confusion, such a whirl! But I will become historical, and quietly relate my doings, else you will learn nothing about me.

* * *

Could you but see the highly respectable, fog-enveloped street and hear the deplorable voice with which a beggar down there pours forth his ditty (he will soon be drowned out by the street-vendors) and could you suspect that from here to the City is a three-quarters-of-an-hour drive, and that along the whole way, at every cross street of which one catches a glimpse, the uproar is the same, if not far greater, and that one has then traversed only about a quarter of residential London, then you might understand how it is that I am half distracted. But I must be historical!

WILLIAM BLAKE
(1757–1827)

from *Jerusalem*

Hampstead, Highgate, Finchley, Hendon, Muswell hill rage loud
Before Bromion's iron Tongs & glowing Poker reddening fierce;
Hertfordshire glows with fierce Vegetation; in the Forests
The Oak frowns terrible, the Beech & Ash & Elm enroot
Among the Spiritual fires; loud the Corn-fields thunder along,
The Soldier's fife, the Harlot's shriek, the Virgin's dismal groan,
The Parent's fear, the Brother's jealousy, the Sister's curse,
Beneath the Storms of Theotormon, & the thund'ring Bellows
Heaves in the hand of Palamabron, who in London's darkness
Before the Anvil watches the bellowing flames: thundering
The Hammer loud rages in Rintrah's strong grasp, swinging loud
Round from heaven to earth, down falling with heavy blow
Dead on the Anvil, where the red hot wedge groans in pain.
He quenches it in the black trough of his Forge: London's River
Feeds the dread Forge, trembling & shuddering along the Valleys.

AMY CLAMPITT
(1920–92)

London Inside and Outside

Looked back on happily, the ivy-hung,
back-wall-embowered garden of our
pied-à-terre and domicile in Chelsea
seems oddly like some dream of living
halfway down the well that sheltered
Charles Dodgson's Elsie, Lacie
and Tillie – with those geraniums
in urns, that lily-of-the-valley
bed not quite in bloom, those churring
ringdoves, those thrushes murderously
foraging for earthworms: an exterior
so self-contained, a view so inward
that though at night we'd note
faint window-glimmerings eclipsed by ivy,
we seemed to have no neighbors either
to spy on or be spied on by.

Those strolls at dusk, the sidewalks
puddled underfoot, the streetlamps
an aloof processional (a footfall
once or twice, then silence)
at the hour not of the pulling down
of shades but rather of the drawing
in of curtains on their rods, with
an occasional small, to-be-savored
lapse – the glimpse in solitude
of the young woman meditatively
taking off her coat: or of
the table laid, the TV
in the dining room tuned to the news,
a South-Sea-bubble porthole open
on the mysteries of domicile,
of anchorage, of inside-outside!

21

The night we took the Underground
to Covent Garden, we found the foyer
at the opera a roofed-in waterfall
of crystal, the staircase we sat on
at the interval to eat our ices
carpet-luscious (even to the shod
sole) as a bed of crimson mosses,
the rose-red lampshades erotic
as hothouse hibiscus. Floated
overhead, a firmament of gilt
and turquoise; as that goes dim,
beneath the royal monogram the bell jar
of illusion lifts, and yet again
we're inside-outside: Norina's
rooftop vista (the duenna
furiously knitting) of a hot-bright
Bay of Naples. In the obscurity
of our neck-craning balcony, we
snuggled undetected. Outside there waited
a shivering, rain-speckled exodus among
dark gardens of the inevitable
umbrellas going up.

FLEUR ADCOCK
(b. 1934)

Londoner

Scarcely two hours back in the country
and I'm shopping in East Finchley High Road
in a cotton skirt, a cardigan, jandals –
or flipflops as people call them here,
where February's winter. Aren't I cold?
The neighbours in their overcoats are smiling
at my smiles and not at my bare toes:
they know me here.
                    I hardly know myself,
yet. It takes me until Monday evening,
walking from the office after dark
to Westminster Bridge. It's cold, it's foggy,
the traffic's as abominable as ever,
and there across the Thames is County Hall,
that uninspired stone body, floodlit.
It makes me laugh. In fact, it makes me sing.

2

UNREAL CITY

The fields from Islington to Marybone,
To Primrose Hill and Saint John's Wood,
Were builded over with pillars of gold;
And there Jerusalem's pillars stood.

William Blake, *Jerusalem*

T. S. ELIOT
(1888–1965)

The Burial of the Dead

   Unreal City,
Under the brown fog of a winter dawn,
A crowd flowed over London Bridge, so many,
I had not thought death had undone so many.
Sighs, short and infrequent, were exhaled,
And each man fixed his eyes before his feet.
Flowed up the hill and down King William Street,
To where Saint Mary Woolnoth kept the hours
With a dead sound on the final stroke of nine.
There I saw one I knew, and stopped him, crying: 'Stetson!
'You who were with me in the ships at Mylae!
'That corpse you planted last year in your garden,
'Has it begun to sprout! Will it bloom this year?
'Or has the sudden frost disturbed its bed?
'Oh keep the Dog far hence, that's friend to men,
'Or with his nails he'll dig it up again!
'You! hypocrite lecteur! – mon semblable, – mon frère!'

from *The Waste Land*

WILLIAM BLAKE
(1757–1827)

from *Jerusalem*

I behold London; a Human awful wonder of God!
He says: 'Return, Albion, return! I give myself for thee:
My Streets are my Ideas of Imagination.
Awake, Albion, awake! and let us awake up together.
My Houses are Thoughts; my Inhabitants Affections,
The children of my thoughts, walking within my blood-vessels,
Shut from my nervous form which sleeps upon the verge of
    Beulah
In dreams of darkness, while my vegetating blood in veiny pipes,
Rolls dreadful thro' the Furnaces of Los, and the Mills of Satan.
For Albion's sake and for Jerusalem thy Emanation
I give myself, and these my brethren give themselves for Albion.'

So spoke London, immortal Guardian! I heard in Lambeth's
    shades:
In Felpham I heard and saw the Vision of Albion:
I write in South Molton Street, what I both see and hear
In regions of Humanity, in London's opening streets.

★   ★   ★

There is a Grain of Sand in Lambeth that Satan cannot find,
Nor can his Watch Fiends find it: 'tis translucent & has many
    Angles:
But he who finds it will find Oothoon's palace; for within,
Opening into Beulah, every angle is a lovely heaven
But should the Watch Fiends find it, they would call it Sin
And lay its Heavens & their inhabitants in blood of punishment.

★   ★   ★

'Highgate's heights & Hampstead's, to Poplar, Hackney & Bow,
'To Islington & Paddington & the Brook of Albion's River.
'We builded Jerusalem as a City & a Temple; from Lambeth
'We began our Foundations, lovely Lambeth! O lovely Hills

'Of Camberwell, we shall behold you no more in glory &
    pride,
'For Jerusalem lies in ruins & the Furnaces of Los are builded
    there.
'You are now shrunk up to a narrow Rock in the midst of the
    Sea;
'But here we build Babylon on Euphrates, compell'd to build
'And to inhabit, our Little-ones to clothe in armour of the gold
'Of Jerusalem's Cherubims & to forge them swords of her Altars.
'I see London, blind & age bent, begging thro' the Streets
'Of Babylon, led by a child; his tears run down his beard.

ALAN BROWNJOHN
(b. 1931)

The Cities

I was born in one of London's various cities.
And travelled through others that I never could
Explore except from an upper-deck front seat,
In the time I was a nineteen-thirties child.

Grown up from that, I learned to use the maps
Of more of them; but forgot to understand
What my own city told me, that outdated place
I thought I had left behind. When I go back now,

I can feel inside myself something waiting, hidden
By time and the Red Routes and the roundabouts,
By the deaths of faces I grew up among
And lost the strength to know.   I like to think

– Or fear to think it – that one day my city will
Disclose itself, its faces reclaim their focus,
Its culverted rivers flood the hypermarkets,
The cinema organs rise through the motorways.

W. H. AUDEN
(1907–73)

The Londoners
[1938?]

A city is the creation of the human will.
Upon the natural life of the field,
Determined by the radiations of the sun and the swing of the
  seasons,
Man imposes a human space,
A human skyline,
A human time,
A human order.
A city is not a flower.
It does not grow right by itself.
A human creation,
It needs the human powers of intelligence and forethought.
Without them it becomes only a monument to human greed
Out of control, like a malignant tumour,
Stunting and destroying life.

★ ★ ★

And the parks and open spaces inside the city:
Battersea Park and Bostall Woods,
Clapham and Tooting Commons,
Peckham Rye and the island gardens of Poplar,
The Regent Canal and the Round Pond of respectable
  Kensington,
And pram-covered Hampstead.
Areas of light and air where the bands boom on Sunday
  afternoons.
Space for strollers,
        Liberty for lovers,
        Room for rest,
Places for play.

★ ★ ★

It belongs to them, to make it what they choose
For democracy means faith in the ordinary man and woman,
    in the decency of average human nature.
Here then in London build the city of the free.

3

THE WEATHER IN THE STREETS

The banks of the Thames are clouded! the ancient porches of
   Albion are
Darken'd!

William Blake, *Jerusalem*

JONATHAN SWIFT
(1667–1745)

A Description of a City Shower

Careful observers may foretell the hour
(By sure prognostics) when to dread a show'r:
While rain depends, the pensive cat gives o'er
Her frolics, and pursues her tail no more.
Returning home at night, you'll find the sink
Strike your offended sense with double stink.
If you be wise, then go not far to dine,
You spend in coach-hire more than save in wine.
A coming show'r your shooting corns presage,
Old aches throb, your hollow tooth will rage.
Sauntering in coffee-house is Dullman seen;
He damns the climate, and complains of spleen.

Mean while the south rising with dabbled wings,
A sable cloud a-thwart the welkin flings,
That swill'd more liquor than it could contain,
And like a drunkard gives it up again.
Brisk Susan whips her linen from the rope,
While the first drizzling show'r is born aslope,
Such is that sprinkling which some careless quean
Flirts on you from her mop, but not so clean.
You fly, invoke the Gods; then turning, stop
To rail; she singing, still whirls on her mop.
Not yet, the dust had shunn'd th' unequal strife,
But aided by the wind, fought still for life;
And wafted with its foe by violent gust,
'Twas doubtful which was rain, and which was dust.
Ah! where must needy poet seek for aid,
When dust and rain at once his coat invade;
Sole coat, where dust cemented by the rain.
Erects the nap, and leaves a cloudy stain.

Now in contiguous drops the flood comes down,
Threat'ning with deluge this *devoted* town.
To shops in crowds the dagled females fly,
Pretend to cheapen goods, but nothing buy.
The templer spruce, while ev'ry spout's a-broach,
Stays till 'tis fair, yet seems to call a coach.
The tuck'd-up sempstress walks with hasty strides,
While streams run down her oil'd umbrella's sides.
Here various kinds by various fortunes led,
Commence acquaintance underneath a shed.
Triumphant Tories, and desponding Whigs,
Forget their feuds, and join to save their wigs.
Boxed in a chair the beau impatient sits,
While spouts run clatt'ring o'er the roof by fits;
And ever and anon with frightful din
The leather sounds, he trembles from within.
So when Troy chair-men bore the wooden steed,
Pregnant with Greeks, impatient to be freed,
(Those bully Greeks, who, as the moderns do,
Instead of paying chair-men, run them thro').
Laoco'n struck the outside with his spear,
And each imprison'd hero quak'd for fear.

Now from all parts the swelling kennels flow,
And bear their trophies with them as they go:
Filth of all hues and odours seem to tell
What streets they sail'd from, by the sight and smell.
They, as each torrent drives, with rapid force
From Smithfield, or St Pulchre's shape their course,
And in huge confluent join at Snow-Hill Ridge,
Fall from the conduit prone to Holborn-Bridge.
Sweepings from butchers' stalls, dung, guts, and blood,
Drown'd puppies, stinking sprats, all drench'd in mud,
Dead cats and turnip-tops come tumbling down the flood.

ROBERT BRIDGES
(1844–1930)

London Snow

When men were all asleep the snow came flying,
In large white flakes falling on the city brown,
Stealthily and perpetually settling and loosely lying,
    Hushing the latest traffic of the drowsy town;
Deadening, muffling, stifling its murmurs failing;
Lazily and incessantly floating down and down:
    Silently sifting and veiling road, roof and railing;
Hiding difference, making unevenness even,
Into angles and crevices softly drifting and sailing.
    All night it fell, and when full inches seven
It lay in the depth of its uncompacted lightness,
The clouds blew off from a high and frosty heaven;
    And all woke earlier for the unaccustomed brightness
Of the winter dawning, the strange unheavenly glare:
The eye marvelled – marvelled at the dazzling whiteness;
    The ear hearkened to the stillness of the solemn air;
No sound of wheel rumbling nor of foot falling,
And the busy morning cries came thin and spare.
    Then boys I heard, as they went to school, calling,
They gathered up the crystal manna to freeze
Their tongues with tasting, their hands with snowballing;
    Or rioted in a drift, plunging up to the knees;
Or peering up from under the white-mossed wonder,
'O look at the trees!' they cried, 'O look at the trees!'
    With lessened load a few carts creak and blunder,
Following along the white deserted way,
A country company long dispersed asunder:
    When now already the sun, in pale display
Standing by Paul's high dome, spread forth below
His sparkling beams, and awoke the stir of the day.

For now doors open, and war is waged with the snow;
And trains of sombre men, past tale of number,
Tread long brown paths, as toward their toil they go:
But even for them awhile no cares encumber
Their minds diverted; the daily word is unspoken,
The daily thoughts of labour and sorrow slumber
At the sight of the beauty that greets them, for the charm
they have broken.

KATHLEEN RAINE
(b. 1908)

London Rain

These diamond spheres
Tainted from poisoned air that blows about the houses,
Each sour raindrop hanging from wire or railings
Yet catches its ray to open the rainbow light
Of heavenly promise before it falls
On sterile ground to moisten the patient moss
That mends with living green
Of Paradise, springing from blown dust in cracks and crevices
For lonely downcast eyes to find a long-ago familiar place.

London Wind

Wind, lifting litter, paper, empty containers, grit,
Even here blows the element of air –
Between post-office and supermarket still the caress
Of earth's breath cool on my face
As gusts in spirals and eddies whirl
Spent leaves from London's plane-trees, to let fall
Perfect forms so lightly poised on a vandalized lot.

CHARLES DICKENS
(1812–70)

from *Bleak House*

CHAPTER 1: In Chancery

LONDON. Michaelmas Term lately over, and the Lord Chancellor sitting in Lincoln's Inn Hall. Implacable November weather. As much mud in the streets, as if the waters had but newly retired from the face of the earth, and it would not be wonderful to meet a Megalosaurus, forty feet long or so, waddling like an elephantine lizard up Holborn Hill. Smoke lowering down from chimney-pots, making a soft black drizzle, with flakes of soot in it as big as full-grown snow-flakes – gone into mourning, one might imagine, for the death of the sun. Dogs, undistinguishable in mire. Horses, scarcely better; splashed to their very blinkers. Foot passengers, jostling one another's umbrellas, in a general infection of ill-temper, and losing their foothold at street-corners, where tens of thousands of other foot passengers have been slipping and sliding since the day broke (if the day ever broke), adding new deposits to the crust upon crust of mud, sticking at those points tenaciously to the pavement, and accumulating at compound interest.

Fog everywhere. Fog up the river, where it flows among green aits and meadows; fog down the river, where it rolls defiled among the tiers of shipping, and the waterside pollutions of a great (and dirty) city. Fog on the Essex marshes, fog on the Kentish heights. Fog creeping into the cabooses of collier-brigs; fog lying out on the yards, and hovering in the rigging of great ships; fog drooping on the gunwales of barges and small boats. Fog in the eyes and throats of ancient Greenwich pensioners, wheezing by the firesides of their wards; fog in the stem and bowl of the afternoon pipe of the wrathful skipper, down in his close cabin; fog cruelly pinching the toes and fingers of his shivering little 'prentice boy on deck. Chance people on the bridges peeping over the parapets into a nether sky of fog, with fog all round them, as if they were up in a balloon, and hanging in the misty clouds.

Gas looming through the fog in divers places in the streets, much as the sun may, from the spongey fields, be seen to loom by husbandman and ploughboy. Most of the shops lighted two hours before their time – as the gas seems to know, for it has a haggard and unwilling look.

The raw afternoon is rawest, and the dense fog is densest, and the muddy streets are muddiest, near that leaden-headed old obstruction, appropriate ornament for the threshold of a leaden-headed old corporation: Temple Bar. And hard by Temple Bar, in Lincoln's Inn Hall, at the very heart of the fog, sits the Lord High Chancellor in his High Court of Chancery.

Never can there come fog too thick, never can there come mud and mire too deep, to assort with the groping and floundering condition which this High Court of Chancery, most pestilent of hoary sinners, holds, this day, in the sight of heaven and earth.

THOMAS HOOD
(1799–1845)

No!

No sun – no moon!
No morn – no noon –
No dawn – no dusk – no proper time of day –
No sky – no earthly view –
No distance looking blue –
No road – no street – no 't'other side the way' –
No end to any Row –
No indications where the Crescents go –
No top to any steeple –
No recognitions of familiar people –
No courtesies for showing 'em –
No knowing 'em! –
No travelling at all – no locomotion,
No inkling of the way- no notion –
'No go'- by land or ocean –
No mail – no post –
No news from any foreign coast –
No Park – no Ring – no afternoon gentility –
No company – no nobility –
No warmth, no cheerfulness, no healthful ease,
No comfortable feel in any member –
No shade, no shine, no butterflies, no bees,
No fruits, no flowers, no leaves, no birds –
November!

ANNA ADAMS
(b. 1926)

A Rainbow over Brewer Street

The sun that shone down Brewer Street
  silvered the falling threads
of tinsel rain that sprinkled wet
  on shop-blinds and bowed heads,

while over-arching Brewer Street,
  above its shady chasm
a flyover of coloured light
  was conjured through the prism

of sunlit rain wrung from the mops
  that polished the blue sky.
In doorways, businessmen and cops
  gave rainbow girls the eye.

4

TRADES AND THE MARKET

Pray'st thou for Riches away away
This is the Throne of Mammon grey

Said I this sure is very odd
I took it to be the Throne of God

Willaim Blake, *Notebook*

★ ★ ★

When Nations grow Old, the Arts grow Cold
And Commerce settles on every Tree

William Blake, *Marginalia, on Reynolds*

GEOFFREY CHAUCER
(c. 1343–1400)

The Cook's Tale

There was a prentice living in our town
Worked in the victualling trade, and he was brown,
Brown as a berry, a proper thick-set fellow
Spruce as a hedgerow finch with tail of yellow.
His hair was black and delicately curled;
He looked so jolly when he danced and twirled
That he was known as Party Peterkin.
He was as full of love, as full of sin
As hives are full of honey, and as sweet.
Lucky the wench that Peter chanced to meet.
At every wedding he would sing and hop
And he preferred the tavern to the shop.
   Whenever any pageant or procession
Came down Cheapside, goodbye to his profession!
He'd leap out of the shop to see the sight
And join the dance and not come back that night.
He gathered round him many of his sort
And made a gang for dancing, song and sport.
They used to make appointments where to meet
For playing dice in such and such a street,
And no apprentice had a touch so nice
As Peter when it came to casting dice.
Yet he was free with money and persisted
In being reckless rather than close-fisted.
Of this his master soon became aware;
Many a time he found the till was bare,
For when apprentices are caught in whirls
Of dancing-parties, dice, and easy girls,
They cost their master's shop a pretty penny;
Little the minstrelsy for him, if any.
Riot and theft can interchange and are
Convertible by fiddle and guitar.
Revels and honesty among the poor
Are pretty soon at strife you may be sure.

This jolly prentice, doing little good,
Stayed with his master through his prenticehood
Though scolded night and morning without fail
And often led with minstrelsy to jail.
But in the end his master, taking thought
While casting up what he had sold and bought,
Hit on a proverb as he sat and pored:
'Throw out a rotten apple from the hoard
Or it will rot the others,' said the tag.
So with a squandering servant; let him brag
And he'll corrupt all servants in the place.
Far better to dismiss him in disgrace.
His master, then, gave Peterkin the sack
With curses and forbade him to come back,
And so this jolly prentice left his shop.
Now let him revel all the night, or stop.
As there's no thief but has a pal or plucker
To help him to lay waste or milk the sucker
From whom he borrows cash or steals instead,
Peter sent round his bundle and his bed
To a young fellow of the self-same sort
Equally fond of revelling, dice and sport,
Whose wife kept shop – but that was just for giving
Her countenance; she tarted for a living . . .

Translated by Geoffrey Grigson

WILLIAM BLAKE
(1757–1827)

The Chimney Sweeper

When my mother died I was very young,
And my father sold me while yet my tongue
Could scarcely cry "'weep! 'weep! 'weep! 'weep!'
So your chimneys I sweep & in soot I sleep.

There's little Tom Dacre, who cried when his head
That curl'd like a lamb's back, was shav'd, so I said,
'Hush Tom never mind it, for when your head's bare,
You know that the soot cannot spoil your white hair.'

And so he was quiet, & that very night,
As Tom was a-sleeping he had such a sight,
That thousands of sweepers, Dick, Joe, Ned, & Jack
Were all of them lock'd up in coffins of black.

And by came an Angel who had a bright key,
And he open'd the coffins & set them all free.
Then down a green plain leaping, laughing, they run,
And wash in a river and shine in the Sun.

Then, naked & white, all their bags left behind,
They rise upon clouds, and sport in the wind;
And the Angel told Tom if he'd be a good boy,
He'd have God for his father, & never want joy.

And so Tom awoke, and we rose in the dark,
And got with our bags & our brushes to work.
Tho' the morning was cold, Tom was happy & warm:
So, if all do their duty, they need not fear harm.

from Songs of Innocence

The Chimney Sweeper

A little black thing among the snow,
Crying ''weep! 'weep!' in notes of woe!
'Where are thy father & mother? say?'
'They are both gone up to the church to pray.

'Because I was happy upon the heath,
'And smil'd among the winter's snow,
'They clothed me in the clothes of death,
'And taught me to sing the notes of woe.

'And because I am happy & dance & sing,
'They think they have done me no injury,
'And are gone to praise God & his Priest & King,
'Who make up a heaven of our misery.'

from *Songs of Experience*

JONATHAN SWIFT
(1667–1745)

Verses made for Women who cry Apples, &c.

APPLES
Come buy my fine wares,
Plums, apples and pears,
A hundred a penny,
In conscience too many,
Come, will you have any;
My children are seven,
I wish them in Heaven,
My husband's a sot,
With his pipe and his pot,
Not a farthing will gain 'em,
And I must maintain 'em.

ASPARAGUS
Ripe 'sparagrass,
    Fit for lad or lass,
To make their water pass:
    O, 'tis pretty picking
    With a tender chicken.

ONIONS
Come, follow me by the smell,
Here's delicate onions to sell,
I promise to use you well.
They make the blood warmer,
You'll feed like a farmer:
For this is ev'ry cook's opinion,
No sav'ry dish without an onion;
But lest your kissing should be spoil'd,
Your onions must be th'roughly boil'd;
    Or else you may spare
    Your mistress a share,
The secret will never be known;
    She cannot discover
    The breath of her lover,
But think it as sweet as her own.

51

OYSTERS

Charming oysters I cry,
My masters come buy,
So plump and so fresh,
So sweet is their flesh,
No Colchester oyster,
Is sweeter and moister,
Your stomach they settle,
And rouse up your mettle,
They'll make you a dad
Of a lass or a lad;
And, madam your wife
They'll please to the life;
Be she barren, be she old,
Be she slut, or be she scold,
Eat my oysters, and lie near her,
She'll be fruitful, never fear her.

HERRINGS

Be not sparing,
Leave off swearing
Buy my herring
Fresh from Malahide,
Better ne'er was tried.
Come eat 'em with pure fresh butter and mustard,
Their bellies are soft, and as white as a custard,
Come, six-pence a dozen to get me some bread,
Or, like my own herrings, I soon shall be dead.

ORANGES

Come, buy my fine oranges, sauce for your veal,
And charming when squeez'd in a pot of brown ale.
Well roasted, with sugar and wine in a cup,
They'll make a sweet bishop when gentlefolks sup.

JAMES BERRY
(b. 1924)

The Coming of Yams and Mangoes and Mountain Honey

Handfuls hold hidden sunset
stuffing up bags
and filling up the London baskets.
Caribbean hills have moved and come.

Sun's alphabet drops out of branches.
Coconuts are big brown Os,
pimentoberries little ones.
Open up papaw like pumpkin you get
the brightness of macaw.

Breadfruit a green football,
congo-peas like tawny pearls,
mango soaked in sunrise,
avocado is a fleshy green.

Colours of sun, stalled in groups,
make market a busy meeting.
The sweetnesses of summer settle smells.

Mints and onions quarrel.
Nutmeg and orange and cinnamon hug
themselves in sun-perfume.

Some of the round bodies shown off
have grown into long shapes.
Others grew fisty and knobbled.
Jars hold black molasses like honey.

And yams the loaves
of earth's big bellies and sun,
plantains too huge to be bananas,
melons too smooth to be pineapples –
chocho, okra, sweetsop, soursop, sorrel –
all are sun flavoured geniuses.

Nights once lit the growing lots
with fields of squinting kitibus.
Winds polished some of the skins cool but warm
when sun drew stripes on fish.

But, here, you won't have a topseat cooing
in peppers, won't hear the nightingale's
notes mixed with lime juice.

Red buses pass for donkeys now.
Posters of pop stars hang by.

Caribbean hills have moved
and come to London
with whole words of the elements.
Just take them and give them
to children, to parents and the old folks.

---

kitibu: the click-beetle, or firefly, with two luminous spots that squint light in
the dark.

THOMAS DE QUINCEY
(1785–1859)

from *Confessions of an English Opium-Eater*

Meantime, what had become of poor Ann? For her I have reserved my concluding words: according to our agreement, I sought her daily, and waited for her every night, so long as I staid in London, at the corner of Titchfield-street. I inquired for her of every one who was likely to know her; and, during the last hours of my stay in London, I put into activity every means of tracing her that my knowledge of London suggested, and the limited extent of my power made possible. The street where she had lodged I knew, but not the house; and I remembered at last some account which she had given me of ill treatment from her landlord, which made it probable that she had quitted those lodgings before we parted. She had few acquaintance; most people, besides, thought that the earnestness of my inquiries arose from motives which moved their laughter, or their slight regard; and others, thinking I was in chase of a girl who had robbed me of some trifles, were naturally and excusably indisposed to give me any clue to her, if, indeed, they had any to give. Finally, as my despairing resource, on the day I left London I put into the hands of the only person who (I was sure) must know Ann by sight, from having been in company with us once or twice, an address to — in — shire, at that time the residence of my family. But, to this hour, I have never heard a syllable about her. This, amongst such troubles as most men meet with in this life, has been my heaviest affliction. – If she lived, doubtless we must have been sometimes in search of each other, at the very same moment, through the mighty labyrinths of London; perhaps, even within a few feet of each other – a barrier no wider in a London street, often amounting in the end to a separation for eternity! During some years, I hoped that she *did* live; and I suppose that, in the literal and unrhetorical use of the word *myriad*, I may say that on my different visits to London, I have looked into many, many myriads of female faces, in the hope of meeting her. I should know her again amongst a thousand, if I saw her for a moment; for, though not handsome, she had a sweet expression of countenance, and a peculiar and graceful carriage of the head. – I sought her, I have said, in hope. So it was for years; but now I should fear to see her; and her cough, which grieved me when I parted with her, is now my consolation. I now wish to see her no longer; but think of her, more gladly, as one long since laid in the grave; in the grave, I would hope, of a Magdalen; taken away, before injuries and cruelty had blotted out and transfigured her ingenuous nature, or the brutalities of ruffians had completed the ruin they had begun.

CHARLES LAMB
(1775–1834)

The Praise of Chimney-Sweepers

I like to meet a sweep – understand me – not a grown sweeper – old chimney-sweepers are by no means attractive – but one of those tender novices, blooming through their first nigritude, the maternal washings not quite effaced from the cheek – such as come forth with the dawn, or somewhat earlier, with their little professional notes sounding like the *peep-peep* of a young sparrow; or liker to the matin lark should I pronounce them, in their aërial ascents not seldom anticipating the sun-rise?

I have a kindly yearning towards these dim specks – poor blots – innocent blacknesses –

I reverence these young Africans of our own growth – these almost clergy imps, who sport their cloth without assumption; and from their little pulpits (the tops of chimneys), in the nipping air of a December morning, preach a lesson of patience to mankind.

When a child, what a mysterious pleasure it was to witness their operation! to see a chit no bigger than one's-self, enter, one knew not by what process, into what seemed the *fauces Averni* – to pursue him in imagination, as he went sounding on through so many dark stifling caverns, horrid shades! to shudder with the idea that 'now, surely he must be lost for ever!' – to revive at hearing his feeble shout of discovered day-light – and then (O fulness of delight!) running out of doors, to come just in time to see the sable phenomenon emerge in safety, the brandished weapon of his art victorious like some flag waved over a conquered citadel! I seem to remember having been told, that a bad sweep was once left in a stack with his brush, to indicate which way the wind blew. It was an awful spectacle, certainly; not much unlike the old stage direction in Macbeth, where the 'Apparition of a child crowned, with a tree in his hand, rises.'

Reader, if thou meetest one of these small gentry in thy early rambles, it is good to give him a penny, – it is better to give him twopence. If it be starving weather, and to the proper troubles of his hard occupation, a pair of kibed heels (no unusual accompaniment) be superadded, the demand on thy humanity will surely rise to a tester.

The Good Clerk

I have now lying before me that curious book by Daniel Defoe, 'The Complete English Tradesman.' The pompous detail, the studied analysis of every little mean art, every sneaking address, every trick and subterfuge, short of larceny, that is necessary to the tradesman's occupation, with the hundreds of anecdotes, dialogues (in Defoe's liveliest manner) interspersed, all tending to the same amiable purpose, – namely, the sacrificing of every honest emotion of the soul to what he calls the main chance, – if you read it in an *ironical sense*, and as a piece of *covered satire*, make it one of the most amusing books which Defoe ever writ, as much so as any of his best novels. It is difficult to say what his intention was in writing it. It is almost impossible to suppose him in earnest.

★   ★   ★

[The shopkeeper] must have no passions, no fire in his temper; he must be all soft and smooth; nay, if his real temper be naturally fiery and hot, he must show none of it in his shop; he must be a perfect *complete hypocrite*, if he will be a *complete tradesman*.★ It is true, natural tempers are not to be always counterfeited: the man cannot easily be a lamb in his shop, and a lion in himself; but, let it be easy or hard, it must be done, and is done. There are men who have by custom and usage brought themselves to it, that nothing could be meeker and milder than they when behind the counter, and yet nothing be more furious and raging in every other part of life: nay, the provocations they have met with in their shops have so irritated their rage, that they would go upstairs from their shop, and fall into frenzies, and a kind of madness, and beat their heads against the wall, and perhaps mischief themselves, if not prevented, till the violence of it had gotten vent, and the passions abate and cool. I heard once of a shopkeeper that behaved himself thus to such an extreme, that, when he was provoked by the impertinence of the customers beyond what his temper could bear, he would go upstairs and beat his wife, kick his children about like dogs, and be as furious for two or three minutes as a man chained down in Bedlam; and again, when that heat was over, would sit down, and cry faster than

---

★As no qualification accompanies this maxim, it must be understood as the genuine sentiment of the author!

the children he had abused; and, after the fit, he would go down into the shop again, and be as humble, courteous, and as calm, as any man whatever; so absolute a government of his passions had he in the shop, and so little out of it: in the shop, a soulless animal that would resent nothing; and in the family, a madman: in the shop, meek like a lamb; but in the family outrageous, like a Lybian lion. The sum of the matter is, it is necessary for a tradesman to subject himself, by all the ways possible, to his business; *his customers are to be his idols: so far as he may worship idols by allowance, he is to bow down to them, and worship them*; at least, he is not in any way to displease them, or show any disgust or distaste, whatsoever they may say or do. The bottom of all is, that he is intending to get money by them; and it is not for him that gets money to offer the least inconvenience to them by whom he gets it: he is to consider, that, as Solomon says, 'the borrower is servant to the lender'; so the seller is servant to the buyer. What he says on the head of 'Pleasures and Recreations' is not less amusing: 'The tradesman's pleasure should be in his business; his companions should be his books (he means his ledger, waste-book, &c.); and, if he has a family, he makes his *excursions upstairs, and no further*. None of my cautions aim at restraining a tradesman from diverting himself, as we call it, with his fireside, or keeping company with his wife and children.' Liberal allowance! nay, almost licentious and criminal indulgence! But it is time to dismiss this Philosopher of Meanness.

from The Essays of Elia

5

THE POOR AND THE RICH

I see London, blind & age bent, begging thro' the Streets
Of Babylon, led by a child; his tears run down his beard.

William Blake, *Jerusalem*

SAMUEL JOHNSON
(1709–1784)

Poverty in London

. . . By numbers here from shame or censure free,
All crimes are safe, but hated poverty.
This, only this, the rigid law pursues,
This, only this, provokes the snarling Muse;
The sober trader at a tatter'd cloak
Wakes from his dream, and labours for a joke;
With brisker air the silken courtiers gaze,
And turn the varied taunt a thousand ways.
Of all the griefs that harrass the distrest,
Sure the most bitter is a scornful jest;
Fate never wounds more deep the gen'rous heart
Then when a blockhead's insult points the dart.
    Has Heaven reserv'd, in pity to the poor
No pathless waste, or undiscover'd shore?
No secret island in the boundless main
No peaceful desert yet unclaim'd by Spain?
Quick let us rise, the happy seats explore,
And bear oppression's insolence no more.
This mournful truth is ev'ry where confest,
Slow rises worth, by poverty deprest:
But here more slow, where all are slaves to gold,
Where looks are merchandise, and smiles are sold,
Where won by bribes, by flatteries implor'd,
The groom retails the favours of his lord . . .

from *London*

63

WILLIAM BLAKE
(1757–1827)

Holy Thursday

'Twas on a Holy Thursday, their innocent faces clean,
The children walking two & two, in red & blue & green,
Grey-headed beadles walk'd before, with wands as white as snow,
Till into the high dome of Paul's they like Thames' waters flow.

O what a multitude they seem'd, these flowers of London town!
Seated in companies they sit with radiance all their own.
The hum of multitudes was there, but multitudes of lambs,
Thousands of little boys & girls raising their innocent hands.

Now like a mighty wind they raise to heaven the voice of song,
Or like harmonious thunderings the seats of Heaven among.
Beneath them sit the aged men, wise guardians of the poor;
Then cherish pity, lest you drive an angel from your door.

from Songs of Innocence

Holy Thursday

Is this a holy thing to see
In a rich and fruitful land,
Babes reduc'd to misery,
Fed with cold and usurous hand?

Is that trembling cry a song?
Can it be a song of joy?
And so many children poor?
It is a land of poverty!

And their sun does never shine,
And their fields are bleak & bare,
And their ways are fill'd with thorns:
It is eternal winter there.

For where-e'er the sun does shine,
And where-e'er the rain does fall,
Babe can never hunger there,
Nor poverty the mind appall.

from *Songs of Experience*

65

CHARLES DICKENS
(1812–70)

The Little Crossing-Sweeper

Jo lives – that is to say, Jo has not yet died – in a ruinous place, known to the like of him by the name of Tom-all-Alone's. It is a black, dilapidated street, avoided by all decent people; where the crazy houses were seized upon, when their decay was far advanced, by some bold vagrants, who, after establishing their own possession, took to letting them out in lodgings. Now, these tumbling tenements contain, by night, a swarm of misery. As, on the ruined human wretch, vermin parasites appear, so, these ruined shelters have bred a crowd of foul existence that crawls in and out of gaps in walls and boards; and coils itself to sleep, in maggot numbers, where the rain drips in; and comes and goes, fetching and carrying fever, and sowing more evil in its every footprint than Lord Coodle, and Sir Thomas Doodle, and the Duke of Foodle, and all the fine gentlemen in office, down to Zoodle, shall set right in five hundred years – though born expressly to do it.

Twice, lately, there has been a crash and a cloud of dust, like the springing of a mine, in Tom-all-Alone's; and, each time, a house has fallen. These accidents have made a paragraph in the newspapers, and have filled a bed or two in the nearest hospital. The gaps remain, and there are not unpopular lodgings among the rubbish. As several more houses are nearly ready to go, the next crash in Tom-all-Alone's may be expected to be a good one.

This desirable property is in Chancery, of course.

★ ★ ★

'For *I* don't,' says Jo, '*I* don't know nothink.'

It must be a strange state to be like Jo! To shuffle through the streets, unfamiliar with the shapes, and in utter darkness as to the meaning, of those mysterious symbols, so abundant over the shops, and at the corners of streets, and on the doors, and in the windows! To see people read and to see people write, and to see the postmen deliver letters, and not to have the least idea of all that language – to be, to every scrap of it, stone blind and dumb! It must be very puzzling to see the good company going to the churches on Sundays, with their books in their hands, and to think (for perhaps Jo *does* think, at odd times) what does it all mean, and if it means anything to anybody, how comes it that it means nothing to me?

★   ★   ★

Jo comes out of Tom-all-Alone's, meeting the tardy morning which is always late in getting down there, and munches his dirty bit of bread as he comes along. His way lying through many streets, and the houses not yet being open, he sits down to breakfast on the door-step of the Society for the Propagation of the Gospel in Foreign Parts, and gives it a brush when he has finished, as an acknowledgement of the accommodation. He admires the size of the edifice, and wonders what it's all about. He has no idea, poor wretch, of the spiritual destitution of a coral reef in the Pacific, or what it costs to look up the precious souls among the cocoa-nuts and bread-fruit.

He goes to his crossing, and begins to lay it out for the day. The town awakes; the great tee-totum is set up for its daily spin and whirl; all that unaccountable reading and writing, which has been suspended for a few hours, recommences. Jo, and the other lower animals, get on in the unintelligible mess as they can. It is market-day. The blinded oxen, over-goaded, over-driven, never guided, run into wrong places and are beaten out; and plunge, red-eyed and foaming, at stone walls; and often sorely hurt the innocent, and often sorely hurt themselves. Very like Jo and his order; very, very like!

from Bleak House

JOHN DAVIDSON
(1857–1909)

Thirty Bob a Week

I couldn't touch a stop and turn a screw,
    And set the blooming world a-work for me,
Like such as cut their teeth – I hope, like you –
    On the handle of a skeleton gold key;
I cut mine on a leek, which I eat it every week:
    I'm a clerk at thirty bob as you can see.

But I don't allow it's luck and all a toss;
    There's no such thing as being starred and crossed;
It's just the power of some to be a boss.
    And the bally power of others to be bossed.
I face the music, sir; you bet I ain't a cur;
    Strike me lucky if I don't believe I'm lost!

For like a mole I journey in the dark,
    A-travelling along the underground
From my Pillar'd Halls and broad Suburbean Park,
    To come the daily dull official round;
And home again at night with my pipe all alight,
    A-scheming how to count ten bob a pound.

And it's often very cold and very wet,
    And my missis stitches towels for a hunks;
And the Pillar'd Halls is half of it to let –
    Three rooms about the size of travelling trunks.
And we cough, my wife and I, to dislocate a sigh,
    When the noisy little kids are in their bunks.

But you never hear her do a growl or whine,
    For she's made of flint and roses, very odd;
And I've got to cut my meaning rather fine,
    Or I'd blubber, for I'm made of greens and sod:
So p'r'aps we are in Hell for all that I can tell.
    And lost and damn'd and served up hot to God.

I ain't blaspheming, Mr Silver-tongue;
  I'm saying things a bit beyond your art:
Of all the rummy starts you ever sprung,
  Thirty bob a week's the rummiest start!
With your science and your books and your the'ries about spooks,
  Did you ever hear of looking in your heart?

I didn't mean your pocket, Mr, no:
  I mean that having children and a wife,
With thirty bob on which to come and go,
  Isn't dancing to the tabor and the fife:
When it doesn't make you drink, by Heaven! it makes you think,
  And notice curious items about life.

I step into my heart and there I meet
  A god-almighty devil singing small,
Who would like to shout and whistle in the street,
  And squelch the passers flat against the wall;
If the whole world was a cake he had the power to take,
  He would take it, ask for more, and eat it all.

And I meet a sort of simpleton beside,
  The kind that life is always giving beans;
With thirty bob a week to keep a bride
  He fell in love and married in his teens:
At thirty bob he stuck; but he knows it isn't luck:
  He knows the seas are deeper than tureens.

And the god-almighty devil and the fool
  That meet me in the High Street on the strike,
When I walk about my heart a-gathering wool,
  Are my good and evil angels if you like.
And both of them together in every kind of weather
  Ride me like a double-seated bike.

That's rough a bit and needs its meaning curled.
  But I have a high old hot un in my mind –
A most engrugious notion of the world,
  That leaves your lightning 'rithmetic behind –
I give it at a glance when I say 'There ain't no chance,
  Nor nothing of the lucky-lottery kind.'

And it's this way that I make it out to be:
    No fathers, mothers, countries, climates – none;
Not Adam was responsible for me,
    Nor society, nor systems, nary one:
A little sleeping seed, I woke – I did, indeed –
    A million years before the blooming sun.

I woke because I thought the time had come;
    Beyond my will there was no other cause;
And everywhere I found myself at home,
    Because I chose to be the thing I was;
And in whatever shape of mollusc or of ape
    I always went according to the laws.

I was the love that chose my mother out;
    I joined two lives and from the union burst;
My weakness and my strength without a doubt
    Are mine alone for ever from the first:
It's just the very same with a difference in the name
    As 'Thy will be done.' You say it if you durst!

They say it daily up and down the land
    As easy as you take a drink, it's true;
But the difficultest go to understand,
    And the difficultest job a man can do,
Is to come it brave and meek with thirty bob a week,
    And feel that that's the proper thing for you.

It's a naked child against a hungry wolf;
    It's playing bowls upon a splitting wreck;
It's walking on a string across a gulf
    With millstones fore-and-aft about your neck;
But the thing is daily done by many and many a one;
    And we fall, face forward, fighting, on the deck.

WILLIAM OXLEY
(b. 1939)

The Bitter Cry of Outcast London*

Many sank like mud to a river's bottom
More like fin-less fish born floating there

London's forever poor, crying outcasts
still not even now quite shadows of the past

Gone the rookeries of Clerkenwell or St. Giles
Gone 'the Nicol' or 'the Jago'
from the sour and yeasty East End
replaced by monstrous moonlit mansions
tenements better on the inside than out
with neighbourly landings and superior plumbing.

Great the struggle of a few compassionate:
'Uncle Sam' Peabody or Octavia Hill,
heroine to countless Victorian poor,
who raised awareness of the degradation
of living in poverty-poisoned rooms,
sheltering but not sustaining ten or more –
where love's inertia soon turned to hate.

The Bitter Cry of Outcast London
echoed round the wealthy walls of Westminster
and along the silent streets of print.
It helped clear the slums but that was all.
It needs another world maybe to put injustice right?

Yet no picture would be complete
that did not tell of how caged birds
sold song to streets of shame,
song of irrepressible joy for many takers:
joy that would often break
on hearts even in suffocating rags.

---

*Title of a famous nineteenth-century pamphlet.

CHARLES LAMB
(1775–1834)

A Complaint of the Decay of Beggars, in the Metropolis

The all-sweeping besom of societarian reformation – your only modern Alcides' club to rid the time of its abuses – is uplift with many-handed sway to extirpate the last fluttering tatters of the bugbear MENDICITY from the metropolis. Scrips, wallets, bags – staves, dogs, and crutches – the whole mendicant fraternity, with all their baggage, are fast posting out of the purlieus of this eleventh persecution. From the crowded crossing, from the corners of steets and turnings of alleys, the parting Genius of Beggary is 'with sighing sent.'

I do not approve of this wholesale going to work, this impertinent crusado, or *bellum ad exterminationem*, proclaimed against a species. Much good might be sucked from these Beggars.

They were the oldest and the honourablest form of pauperism. Their appeals were to our common nature; less revolting to an ingenuous mind than to be a suppliant to the particular humours or caprice of any fellow-creature, or set of fellow-creatures, parochial or societarian. Theirs were the only rates uninvidious in the levy, ungrudged in the assessment.

There was a dignity springing from the very depth of their desolation; as to be naked is to be so much nearer to the being a man, than to go in livery.

★ ★ ★

Pauperism, pauper, poor man, are expressions of pity, but pity alloyed with contempt. No one properly contemns a Beggar. Poverty is a comparative thing, and each degree of it is mocked by its 'neighbour grice.' Its poor rents and comings-in are soon summed up and told. Its pretences to property are almost ludicrous. Its pitiful attempts to save excite a smile. Every scornful companion can weigh his trifle-bigger purse against it. Poor man reproaches poor man in the street with impolitic mention of his condition, his own being a shade better, while the rich pass by and jeer at both. No rascally comparative insults a Beggar, or thinks of weighing purses with him. He is not in the scale of comparison. He is not under the measure of property. He confessedly hath none, any more than a dog or a sheep. No one twitteth him with ostentation above his means. No one accuses him of pride, or upbraideth him with mock humility. None jostle with him for the wall, or pick quarrels for precedency. No wealthy neighbour seeketh to eject him from his tenement. No man sues him. No man goes to law with him. If I were not the independent gentleman that I am, rather than I would be a retainer to the great, a led captain, or a poor relation, I would choose, out of the delicacy and true greatness of my mind, to be a Beggar.

Rags, which are the reproach of poverty, are the Beggar's robes, and graceful *insignia* of his profession, his tenure, his full dress, the suit in which he is expected to show himself in public. He is never out of the fashion, or limpeth awkwardly behind it. He is not required to put on court mourning. He weareth all colours, fearing none. His costume hath undergone less change than the Quaker's. He is the only man in the universe who is not obliged to study appearances. The ups and downs of the world concern him no longer. He alone continueth in one stay. The price of stock or land affecteth him not. The fluctuations of agricultural or commercial prosperity touch him not, or at worst but change his customers. He is not expected to become bail or surety for any one. No man troubleth him with questioning his religion or politics. He is the only free man in the universe.

from *Essays of Elia*

ANNE STEVENSON
(b. 1933)

Cashpoint Charlie

My office, my crouch, is by the Piccadilly cashpoint where
Clients of the Hong Kong and Shanghai Banking Co.
Facilitate my study of legs as they ebb and flow;
Legs, and the influence of sex and wealth on footwear.

The human foot – wedge-shaped, a mini torso –
Used to be, like the monkey's, toed for zipping
Quickly through jungles. Just how prehensile gripping
Got to be a closed shop for hands I'll never know.

Anyhow, feet are in jail now, shoes' prisoners,
Inviting comparison, ladies, with steel-tipped bullets,
And sadly, gentlemen, with coffins. My tiptop favourites
Are Dr Martin's hammer-like hoofs and laceless trainers.

It's a proved fact that the shabbily shod give more.
Like knee-slashed jeans give more than knife-creased trousers.
And shivering junkies more than antique browsers.
What? Thanks to a glitch in the chem lab (not a war)

I'm legless. Or as good as . . . it all depends
On where you poke and what you count as me.
To 'rise' I use a crutch. It helps the money,
And, like my filthy sleeping bag, offends

Your everyday dainty British git just bad enough
To make him pull his Balaclava face
Hard down over his sweet guilt. I make my case:
OK, if you hate me, you have to hate yourself,

And think it steady at him. Nothing's said, of course.
They never meet your eyes, not even the women
Yanking at their big-eyed kids like I was poison,
And then, with a tight look, opening their purse.

It's crazy, but I love them . . . it . . . taking the piss.
If that old guy, that Greek philosopher in his barrel,
Could see me now, in my sleeping bag, beside a hole
In a wall that spits out money, he'd be envious.

U. A. FANTHORPE
(b. 1929)

Counting Song

One man and his dog
Went to mow a meadow.

Not always the same dog,
But the man looks the same, disposable,
Scrapped. Hungerford Bridge his meadow.

This is the city we come to when we're young,
With the golden pavements. Where office-workers whisk
Like weir-water over zebras; where 15s and 77s
Snuffle down bus lanes, showy as heralds.

One woman and a baby

Probably borrowed, we say, not looking,
Moving on. We need to move on.
Our shoes are embarrassed. Our shoes are what she sees.

There's less of sky, now the great Lego thumbs
Angle their vacant heads into the gullspace,
But the saints watch us, Martin the beggars' friend,
Bride in her wedding-cake hat, and Paul,
Skywise and circumspect, sitting out centuries
Under his helmet, Thames washing past,
Refusing to run softly.

One gran and her bottle
Have given up on mowing.

These are waste people, grazing in litterbins,
Sleeping in cardboard, swaddled in broadsheets
And Waitrose plastic bags, who will not be recycled,
Must lie where they fall.

These are the heirs, the true Londoners,
Who work in this stern meadow. The others
Are on their way to somewhere else:
Statesmen and filmstars, remote, chauffeur-driven;
Volatile journalists, folding themselves in taxis,
As homegoers fold themselves into introspection
And the *Evening Standard*.

Written on Hungerford Bridge in letters of chalk:
Save Our Earth. Save Twyford Down.

Save Earth. Save Twyford Down. Save every one.

KIT WRIGHT
(b. 1944)

Fortunes of War

I was thinking about her all the way from Troy
   (I slipped town when the Greek Horse showed)
Till at the pub at World's End called the World's End Arms
   I laid down my heavy load,
Then I called her from the pay-phone at the hamburger counter
   At the top of the New King's Road.

I said,
        'Darling Cassandra!
        How could they call you
        The Priestess with the Leastest,
        Deaf, blind, dumb,
        When the Greeks in the Horse
        Were making with the Morse
        And rat-tat-tapping
        On their wooden drum?
        Oh darling Cassandra,
        How could it be?
        Cassandra, Cassandra,
        Speak to me!'

Well, the line was as dodgy as Achilles' heel
   And I couldn't hear a word she said
So by Stamford Bridge I jumped a Number 14
   And I followed where the Fulham Road led
To a grey block of flats in Elm Park Gardens:
   I rang but the bell was dead.

I yelled,
        'Darling Cassandra!
        You've got a visitor!
        Prophetess, scoff at us,
        You've got a right:
        When it comes to women it's

Quite indiscriminate,
Trojan taste,
But you're out of sight
In my view! Cassandra,
Throw me the key!
Cassandra, Cassandra,
Speak to me!'

That's what I said,
Then out of the window she poked her head,
Sighing,

'Slow down, boy.
Easy, feller.
You don't rob the cage till you've
Stuck up the teller. Take it
Easy, babe.
Gentle, child.
War game losers don't drive me wild.
You've got one chance
Or else you're dead.
Tell me, honey, did you bring any bread?'

Well, I thought about that and I thought about a lot
And I stood in the road feeling dumb.
'Slow down, boy' when you've hitched in from Troy?
Now that was a long way to come
To get this shit. Still the truth of it
Was I'd won me a tidy sum
At Troy's Last Stand and a hundred grand
Was riding against my bum.

So:
'Darling Cassandra!
I've got money!
Peeress of Seeresses,
Open the door!
That treasure chest of Priam's
Was flush as Harry Hyams –
Ripped it all off

And a good bit more.
So darling Cassandra,
Stick with me!
Cassandra, Cassandra,
Throw me the key!'

So I went straight up and Mama Cass and me,
   Now we've had our share of luck,
She prophesies the horses and I bet at all the courses
   And we've never yet come unstuck
So we own West London – well, it gives her an interest –
   But sometimes at night I'm struck
By the thought of Troy Town and the big blood apple
   And I think, well, what the fuck

Was *that* all about? That grey ghost Helen?
   Was she what they all died for?
Patroclus? Hector? Achilles? Priam?
   You can call it the luck of the draw,
I suppose. Well, you have to. I'll drink to that.
   Roll on, fortunes of war.

ARTHUR HUGH CLOUGH
(1819–61)

How Pleasant it is to have Money

As I sat at the café, I said to myself,
They may talk as they please about what they call pelf,
They may sneer as they like about eating and drinking,
But help it I cannot, I cannot help thinking,
    How pleasant it is to have money, heigh ho!
    How pleasant it is to have money.

I sit at my table *en grand seigneur*,
And when I have done, throw a crust to the poor;
Not only the pleasure, one's self, of good living,
But also the pleasure of now and then giving.
    So pleasant it is to have money, heigh ho!
    So pleasant it is to have money.

It was but last winter I came up to Town,
 But already I'm getting a little renown;
I make new acquaintance where'er I appear
I am not too shy, and have nothing to fear.
    So pleasant it is to have money, heigh ho!
    So pleasant it is to have money.

I drive through the streets, and I care not a damn;
The people they stare, and they ask who I am;
And if I should chance to run over a cad,
I can pay for the damage if ever so bad.
    So pleasant it is to have money, heigh ho!
    So pleasant it is to have money.

We stroll to our box and look down on the pit,
And if it weren't low should be tempted to spit;
We loll and we talk until people look up,
And when it's half over we go out and sup.
    So pleasant it is to have money, heigh ho!
    So pleasant it is to have money.

The best of the tables and best of the fare –
And as for the others, the devil may care;
It isn't our fault if they dare not afford
To sup like a prince and be drunk as a lord.
   So pleasant it is to have money, heigh ho!
   So pleasant it is to have money.

We sit at our tables and tipple champagne;
Ere one bottle goes, comes another again;
The waiters they skip and they scuttle about,
And the landlord attends us so civilly out.
   So pleasant it is to have money, heigh ho!
   So pleasant it is to have money.

It was but last winter I came up to town,
But already I'm getting a little renown;
I get to good houses without much ado,
Am beginning to see the nobility too.
   So pleasant it is to have money, heigh ho!
   So pleasant it is to have money.

O dear! what a pity they ever should lose it!
For they are the gentry that know how to use it;
So grand and so graceful, such manners, such dinners,
But yet, after all, it is we are the winners.
   So pleasant it is to have money, heigh ho!
   So pleasant it is to have money.

Thus I sat at my table *en grand seigneur,*
And when I had done threw a crust to the poor;
Not only the pleasure, one's self, of good eating,
But also the pleasure of now and then treating.
   So pleasant it is to have money, heigh ho!
   So pleasant it is to have money.

They may talk as they please about what they call pelf,
And how one ought never to think of one's self,
And how pleasures of thought surpass eating and drinking –
My pleasure of thought is the pleasure of thinking
   How pleasant it is to have money, heigh ho!
   How pleasant it is to have money.

A gondola here, and a gondola there,
'Tis the pleasantest fashion of taking the air.
To right and to left; stop, turn, and go yonder,
And let us repeat, o'er the tide as we wander,
   How pleasant it is to have money, heigh ho!
   How pleasant it is to have money.

6

CHURCHES, PALACES AND TOWERS;
KINGS, PRIESTS AND POLITICIANS

And he beheld Jerusalem in Westminster & Marybone
Among the ruins of the Temple . . .

William Blake, *Jerusalem*

WILLIAM BLAKE
(1757–1827)

Albion's Angel

      Albion's Angel rose upon the Stone of Night.
He saw Urizen on the Atlantic;
And his brazen Book
That Kings & Priests had copied on Earth,
Expanded from North to South.

And the clouds & fires pale roll'd round in the night of
    Enitharmon,
Round Albion's cliffs & London's walls: still Enitharmon slept.
Rolling volumes of grey mist involve Churches, Palaces, Towers;
For Urizen unclasp'd his Book, feeding his soul with pity.
The youth of England, hid in gloom, curse the pain'd heavens,
    compell'd
Into the deadly night to see the form of Albion's Angel.
Their parents brought them forth, & aged ignorance preaches,
    canting,
On a vast rock, perceiv'd by those senses that are clos'd from
    thought:

Bleak, dark, abrupt it stands & overshadows London city.
They saw his boney feet on the rock, the flesh consum'd in
    flames;
They saw the Serpent temple lifted above, shadowing the Island
    white;
They heard the voice of Albion's Angel howling in flames of Orc,
Seeking the trump of the last doom.

Above the rest the howl was heard from Westminster louder &
    louder:
The Guardian of the secret codes forsook his ancient mansion,
Driven out by the flames of Orc; his furr'd robes & false locks
Adhered and grew one with his flesh, and nerves & veins shot
    thro' them.
With dismal torment sick, hanging upon the wind, he fled

Groveling along Great George Street thro' the Park gate: all the
    soldiers
Fled from his sight: he drag'd his torments to the wilderness.

Thus was the howl thro' Europe!
For Orc rejoic'd to hear the howling shadows;
But Palamabron shot his lightnings, trenching down his wide
    back;
And Rintrah hung with all his legions in the nether deep.

Enitharmon laugh'd in her sleep to see (O woman's triumph!)
Every house a den, every man bound: the shadows are fill'd
With spectres, and the windows wove over with curses of iron:
Over the doors 'Thou shalt not,' & over the chimneys 'Fear' is
    written:
With bands of iron round their necks fasten'd into the walls
The citizens, in leaden gyves the inhabitants of suburbs
Walk heavy; soft and bent are the bones of villagers.

from *Europe*

PERCY BYSSHE SHELLEY
(1792–1822)

from *Peter Bell the Third*

PART THE THIRD

HELL

I
HELL is a city much like London –
   A populous and a smoky city;
There are all sorts of people undone,
And there is little or no fun done;
   Small justice shown, and still less pity.

II
There is a Castles, and a Canning,
   A Cobbett, and a Castlereagh;
All sorts of caitiff corpses planning
All sorts of cozening for trepanning
   Corpses less corrupt than they.

III
There is a ★ ★ ★, who has lost
   His wits, or sold them, none knows which;
He walks about a double ghost,
And though as thin as Fraud almost –
   Ever grows more grim and rich.

IV
There is a Chancery Court; a King;
   A manufacturing mob; a set
Of thieves who by themselves are sent
Similar thieves to represent;
   An army; and a public debt.

V

Which last is a scheme of paper money
    And means – being interpreted –
'Bees, keep your wax – give us the honey,
And we will plant, while skies are sunny,
    Flowers, which in winter serve instead.'

VI

There is a great talk of revolution –
    And a great chance of despotism –
German soldiers – camps – confusion –
Tumults – lotteries – rage – delusion –
    Gin – suicide – and methodism;

VII

Taxes too, on wine and bread,
    And meat and beer, and tea, and cheese,
From which those patriots pure are fed,
Who gorge before they reel to bed
    The tenfold essence of all these.

VIII

There are mincing women, mewing,
    (Like cats, who *amant misere*[1],)
Of their own virtue, and pursuing
Their gentler sisters to that ruin,
    Without which – what were chastity?[2]

---

[1] One of the attributes in Linnaeus's description of the Cat. To a similar cause
the caterwauling of more than one species of this genus is to be referred; –
except, indeed, that the poor quadruped is compelled to quarrel with its own
pleasures, whilst the biped is supposed only to quarrel with those of others. –
[SHELLEY'S NOTE.]
[2] What would this husk and excuse for a virtue be without its kernal prostitution,
or the kernal prostitution without this husk of a virtue? I wonder the women of
the town do not form an association, like the Society for the Suppression of
Vice, for the support of what may be called the 'King, Church, and
Constitution' of their order. But this subject is almost too horrible for a joke. –
[SHELLEY'S NOTE.]

IX
Lawyers – judges – old hobnobbers
   Are there – bailiffs – chancellors –
Bishops – great and little robbers –
Rhymesters – pamphleteers – stock-jobbers –
   Men of glory in the wars, –

X
Things whose trade is, over ladies
   To lean, and flirt, and stare, and simper,
Till all that is divine in woman
Grows cruel, courteous, smooth, inhuman,
   Crucified 'twixt a smile and whimper.

XI
Thrusting, toiling, wailing, moiling,
   Frowning, preaching – such a riot!
Each with never-ceasing labour,
Whilst he thinks he cheats his neighbour,
   Cheating his own heart of quiet.

XII
And all these meet at levees; –
   Dinners convivial and political, –
Suppers of epic poets; – teas,
Where small talk dies in agonies; –
   Breakfasts professional and critical;

XIII
Lunches and snacks so aldermanic
   That one would furnish forth ten dinners,
Where reigns a Cretan-tonguèd panic,
Lest news Russ, Dutch or Alemannic
   Should make some losers, and some winners; –

XIV
At conversazioni – balls –
   Conventicles – and drawing-rooms –
Courts of law – committees – calls
Of a morning – clubs – book-stalls –
   Churches – masquerades – and tombs.

XV
And this is Hell − and in this smother
  All are damnable and damned;
Each one damning, damns the other;
They are damned by one another,
  By none other are they damned.

LORD BYRON
(1788–1824)

from *Italy versus England*

'England! with all thy faults I love thee still',
   I said at Calais, and have not forgot it;
I like to speak and lucubrate my fill;
   I like the government (but that is not it);
I like the freedom of the press and quill;
   I like the Habeas Corpus (when we've got it);
I like a Parliamentary debate,
Particularly when 'tis not too late;

I like the taxes, when they're not too many;
   I like a seacoal fire, when not too dear;
I like a beef-steak, too, as well as any;
   Have no objection to a pot of beer;
I like the weather – when it is not rainy,
   That is, I like two months of every year.
And so God save the Regent, Church, and King!
Which means that I like all and every thing.

Our standing army, and disbanded seamen,
   Poor's rate, Reform, my own, the nation's debt,
Our little riots just to show we're free men,
   Our trifling bankruptcies in the Gazette,
Our cloudy climate, and our chilly women,
   All these I can forgive, and those forget,
And greatly venerate our recent glories,
And wish they were not owing to the Tories.

THOMAS HARDY
(1840–1928)

The Coronation

At Westminster, hid from the light of day,
Many who once had shone as monarchs lay.

Edward the Pious, and two Edwards more,
The second Richard, Henrys three or four;

That is to say, those who were called the Third,
Fifth, Seventh, and Eighth (the much self-widowered);

And James the Scot, and near him Charles the Second,
And, too, the second George could there be reckoned.

Of women, Mary and Queen Elizabeth,
And Anne, all silent in a musing death;

And William's Mary, and Mary, Queen of Scots,
And consort-queens whose names oblivion blots;

And several more whose chronicle one sees
Adorning ancient royal pedigrees.

– Now, as they drowsed on, freed from Life's old thrall,
And heedless, save of things exceptional,

Said one: 'What means this throbbing thudding sound
That reaches to us here from overground;

'A sound of chisels, augers, planes, and saws,
Infringing all ecclesiastic laws?

'And these tons-weight of timber on us pressed,
Unfelt here since we entered into rest?

'Surely, at least to us, being corpses royal,
A meet repose is owing by the loyal?'

'– Perhaps a scaffold!' Mary Stuart sighed,
'If such still be. It was that way I died.'

'– Ods! Far more like,' said he the many-wived,
'That for a wedding 'tis this work's contrived.'

'Ha-ha! I never would bow down to Rimmon,
But I had a rare time with those six women!'

'Not all at once?' gasped he who loved confession.
'Nay, nay!' said Hal. 'That would have been transgression.'

'– They build a catafalque here, black and tall,
Perhaps,' mused Richard, 'for some funeral?'

And Anne chimed in: 'Ah, yes: it may be so!'
'Nay!' squeaked Eliza. 'Little you seem to know –

'Clearly 'tis for some crowning here in state
As they crowned us at our long bygone date;

'Though we'd no such a power of carpentry,
But let the ancient architecture be;

'If I were up there where the parsons sit,
In one of my gold robes, I'd see to it!'

'But you are not,' Charles chuckled. 'You are here,
And never will know the sun again, my dear!'

'Yea,' whispered those whom no one had addressed:
'With slow, sad march, amid a folk distressed,
We were brought here, to take our dusty rest.

'And here, alas, in darkness laid below,
We'll wait and listen, and endure the show. . .
Clamour dogs kingship; afterwards not so!'

A Refusal

Said the grave Dean of Westminster:
Mine is the best minster
Seen in Great Britain,
As many have written:
So therefore I cannot
Rule here if I ban not
Such liberty-taking
As movements for making
Its grayness environ
The memory of Byron,
Which some are demanding
Who think them of standing,
But in my own viewing
Require some subduing
For tendering suggestions
On Abbey-wall questions
That must interfere here
With my proper sphere here,
And bring to disaster
This fane and its master,
Whose dict is but Christian
Though nicknamed Philistian.

A lax Christian charity –
No mental clarity
Ruling its movements
For fabric improvements –
Demands admonition
And strict supervision
When bent on enshrining
Rapscallions, and signing
Their names on God's stonework,
As if like His own work
Were their lucubrations:
And passed is my patience
That such a creed-scorner
(Not mentioning horner)
Should claim Poet's Corner.

'Tis urged that some sinners
Are here for worms' dinners
Already in person;
That he could not worsen
The walls by a name mere
With men of such fame here.
Yet nay; they but leaven
The others in heaven
In just true proportion,
While more mean distortion.

'Twill next be expected
That I get erected
To Shelley a tablet
In some niche or gablet.
Then – what makes my skin burn,
Yea, forehead to chin burn –
That I ensconce Swinburne!

August 1924

WILLIAM BLAKE
(1757–1827)

from *Jerusalem*

I stood among my valleys of the south,
And saw a flame of fire, even as a Wheel
Of fire surrounding all the heavens: it went
From west to east against the current of
Creation, and devour'd all things in its loud
Fury & thundering course round heaven & earth.
By it the Sun was roll'd into an orb;
By it the Moon faded into a globe,
Travelling thro' the night; for from its dire
And restless fury Man himself shrunk up
Into a little root a fathom long.
And I asked a Watcher & a Holy-One
Its Name: he answer'd, 'It is the Wheel of Religion.'
I wept & said: 'Is this the law of Jesus,
This terrible devouring sword turning every way?'
He answer'd, 'Jesus died because he strove
Against the current of this Wheel: its Name
Is Caiaphas, the dark Preacher of Death,
Of sin, of sorrow & of punishment,
Opposing Nature. It is Natural Religion.
But Jesus is the bright Preacher of Life,
Creating Nature from this fiery Law
By self-denial & forgiveness of Sin.
Go, therefore, cast out devils in Christ's name!
Heal thou the sick of spiritual disease!
Pity the evil; for thou art not sent
To smite with terror & with punishments
Those that are sick, like to the Pharisees,
Crucifying, & encompassing sea & land
For proselytes to tyranny & wrath.
But to the Publicans & Harlots go!
Teach them True Happiness, but let no curse
Go forth out of thy mouth to blight their peace;
For Hell is open'd to Heaven: thine eyes beheld
The dungeons burst, & the Prisoners set free.'

7

THE RIVER THAMES

> London's River
> Feeds the dread Forge, trembling and shuddering along the Valleys.

> William Blake, *Jerusalem*

GLYN MAXWELL
(b. 1962)

The Fires by the River

Just say you went beside the fires by the river,
in neither night nor day, insofar as
violet and lime were the shades of the air that
    steamed or anchored over
the slurping water, and this was the River Thames
    you somehow knew it.

And people had turned to people of those days,
though moreso, now you walked and heard
the actual cursing, the splattered effluents,
    not far from you in the rose-
grey coloured mud that sloped to the pale Thames
    to be its banks.

Just say the place was a mezzanine or less
up from hell, and who wasn't a thug was a child.
And there was a drug called drug, and a drug that went
    by day in a blue guise;
and there was a boat of cocktailers on the Thames
    staring at this point –

at lolling homes, and clapboard warehouses
shot with mice or riddled with the likes
of Monks and Sikes, who mutter by the wharf –
    skin-crawling passages –
all, just say so, that was real as the Thames
    is, by any life:

what would you do with your clean hands and drowned
feet in the place? Remove them to a room?
Remove them to a room. And sit, forget
    the city-licking sound
of water moving slowly through the Thames
    like years in thought.

London Bridge

London Bridge
Is broken down,
Dance over my Lady Lee,
London Bridge
Is broken down,
With a gay Lady.

How shall we build
It up again,
Dance over my Lady Lee.
How shall we build
It up again,
With a gay Lady.

Build it up with
Gravel, and Stone,
Dance over my Lady Lee.
Build it up with
Gravel, and Stone,
With a gay Lady.

Gravel, and Stone
Will wash away,
Dance over my Lady Lee.
Gravel, and Stone,
Will wash away,
With a gay Lady.

Build it up with
Iron, and Steel,
Dance over my Lady Lee.
Build it up with
Iron, and Steel,
With a gay Lady.

Iron, and Steel,
Will bend, and Bow,
Dance over my Lady Lee.
Iron, and steel,
Will bend, and Bow,
With a gay Lady.

Build it up with
Silver, and Gold,
Dance over my Lady Lee.
Build it up with
Silver, and Gold,
With a gay Lady.

Silver, and Gold,
Will be stolen away,
Dance over my Lady Lee.
Silver, and Gold,
Will be stolen away,
With a gay Lady.

Then we'll set
A Man to Watch,
Dance over my Lady Lee.
Then we'll set
A Man to Watch
With a gay Lady.

BENJAMIN ZEPHANIAH
(b. 1958)

City River Blues

Went to the river
Seeking inspiration,
Saw dead fish floating
Dead men boating
And condoms galore.

Sat by the river
Wondering,
From where cometh
Dat bloody smell,
For if I waz wize
And I could tell
The world would know.

This is our river
It runs through our lives
This is our river
Our shit-coloured river,
It's had it
But it's ours.

This river speaks
Every boot had a body
Every shirt had a friend,
And the old boys
Say they shall all meet
Where every river ends.

Here by this river
Joe Public wrote songs
And ships came
From far away,
Capitalism lived here,
Ships left from here,
To cheat someone,
Somewhere.

This river is on the map
The Queen came here,
The King came here,
Hitler bombed it,
Joe Bloggs bombed it,
A hundred factories
Bomb it every day,
But this river won't go away,
They say.

Went to the river
Seeking inspiration,
Got eco-depression,
Got stopped and searched,
Got called a coon,
Got damned lungs,
Got city river blues.

VERNON WATKINS
(1906–67)

Ballad of the Two Tapsters

Two tapsters traded on Thames's side
When the tide of Thames ran dry.
Their swaggering barrels were big with pride,
But the wine was hard to buy.

They had corks and taps and a counter of wood
But the running wine was gone.
'The old moon's money has gone for good,
But the new moon has not shone.'

'I saw her shining, I saw her shine,'
A tapping beggar cried.
'She carried her fortune, I made it mine,
And sleep upon Thames's side.'

He told how he slept and saw in the mud
The gold and the silver lie,
And a great round barrel, huge as a flood,
Through a corner of his starved eye.

He had watched men trundle it out of the rut
And over a plank; it fell.
He heard the wine run into the butt
As the sea runs into a shell.

Two tapsters traded on Thames's side,
But the trade in the wine went ill.
They were down to their last white penny;
There were shadows and dust in the till.

'O where can we get new wine to sell,
And where can we get it soon?'
'Our barrels are dry as a swollen cork,
Though round as the round full moon.'

They fetched an empty barrel,
They rolled it upon its side.
They propped it against the window-sill
And they pushed the window wide.

Just as the dark came stealing
And the moon rose white and still,
They laid it high on its rolling rim
And left it there to fill.

In a room of fragile moonlight
Under a cask they hide,
And they soon hear mermaids singing
Like drowned men under the tide.

Asleep like rats in the yellow straw,
They dream of a sinking ship,
White horses, a wake, then slipping,
A waggoner cracking his whip.

Now from the window leaking
The flood of light seeps in.
They hear the rattle of wheels on the street
But not one rap at the Inn.

Then up leaps the younger, and leaning
Out of the window, cries:
'Here comes old Beatwind driving
With the glint of gold in his eyes.'

'O where are you going to, Beatwind?'
'To Putney's market of wine.'
'And have you got a corner on that cart of yours
For a butt or a barrel of mine?'

'What wine would it be that you might sell,
And how shall you pay the fee,
Who are banned from the vineyards of Rhine, Moselle,
Champagne and Burgundy?

O what have you got in that barrel?'
He gave them a bargaining frown.
'It will cost you the coats on your bankrupt backs
To get this barrel to town.'

I dreamed last night of a dancing-girl
And the bands on her arms were gold,
But the bands on her ankles were silver:
O what may the great cask hold?

Two tapsters laugh in the sunlight,
In the Winter sunlight cold.
'Now, waggoner, wager your cart and horse,
Here's a barrel your men won't hold.'

Then two men tried to take it,
And four, and six men tried,
But the strongest sinews seemed like straw
That floats on Atlantic's side.

I dreamed last night of a dancing-girl
And the bands on her arms were gold,
But the bands on her ankles were silver:
O what may the great cask hold?

Be warned, you Thames-side traders,
If gambling men you be,
You cannot bend to the shores of the world
Or strive with the great dark sea.

ANNA ADAMS
(b. 1926)

Crossing Hungerford Bridge

At either end of Hungerford's long frieze
of walkers crossing Thames on scissor legs,
reclining figures, draped in blankets, pose
as sculpture: statues with a hand that begs.
The first prompts me to grope for silver pieces
while I stand still and let my heart slow down
after too many stairs. The flood-tide rises
and bears gifts to the richer end of town.
Midway, an old man flutes an Irish jig
in payment for our payment, if we pay;
the statue at the far end, with a dog,
accepts my toll, and I go on my way
the richer, every time I walk this plank,
for more complacency stashed in the bank.

8

MUSEUMS, THEATRES, GALLERIES

All things acted on Earth are seen in the bright Sculptures of
Los's Halls, and every Age renews its powers from these Works,
With every pathetic story possible to happen from Hate or
Wayward Love; & every sorrow & distress is carvèd here;
Every Affinity of Parents, Marriages & Friendships are here
In all their various combinations, wrought with wondrous Art.

William Blake, *Jerusalem*

THOMAS HARDY
(1840–1928)

Christmas in the Elgin Room

BRITISH MUSEUM: EARLY LAST CENTURY

'What is the noise that shakes the night,
   And seems to soar to the Pole-star height?'
     – 'Christmas bells,
     The watchman tells
Who walks this hall that blears us captives with its blight.'

   'And what, then, mean such clangs, so clear?'
   '– 'Tis said to have been a day of cheer,
     And source of grace
     To the human race
Long ere their woven sails winged us to exile here.

   'We are those whom Christmas overthrew
   Some centuries after Pheidias knew
     How to shape us
     And bedrape us
And to set us in Athena's temple for men's view.

   'O it is sad now we are sold –
   We gods! for Borean people's gold,
     And brought to the gloom
     Of this gaunt room
Which sunlight shuns, and sweet Aurore but enters cold.

   'For all these bells, would I were still
   Radiant as on Athenai's Hill.'
     – 'And I, and I!'
     The others sigh,
'Before this Christ was known, and we had men's good will.'

Thereat old Helios could but nod,
Throbbed, too, the Ilissus River-god,
    And the torsos there
    Of deities fair,
Whose limbs were shards beneath some Acropolitan clod:

Demeter too, Poseidon hoar,
Persephone, and many more
    Of Zeus' high breed, –
    All loth to heed
What the bells sang that night which shook them to the core.

1905 and 1926

VIRGINIA WOOLF
(1882–1941)

from *A Room of One's Own*

The scene, if I may ask you to follow me, was now changed. The leaves were still falling, but in London now, not Oxbridge; and I must ask you to imagine a room, like many thousands, with a window looking across people's hats and vans and motor-cars to other windows, and on the table inside the room a blank sheet of paper on which was written in large letters WOMEN AND FICTION, but no more. The inevitable sequel to lunching and dining at Oxbridge seemed, unfortunately, to be a visit to the British Museum. One must strain off what was personal and accidental in all these impressions and so reach the pure fluid, the essential oil of truth. For that visit to Oxbridge and the luncheon and the dinner had started a swarm of questions. Why did men drink wine and women water? Why was one sex so prosperous and the other so poor? What effect has poverty on fiction? What conditions are necessary for the creation of works of art? – a thousand questions at once suggested themselves. But one needed answers, not questions; and an answer was only to be had by consulting the learned and the unprejudiced, who have removed themselves above the strife of tongue and the confusion of body and issued the result of their reasoning and research in books which are to be found in the British Museum. If truth is not to be found on the shelves of the British Museum, where, I asked myself, picking up a notebook and a pencil, is truth?

Thus provided, thus confident and enquiring, I set out in the pursuit of truth. The day, though not actually wet, was dismal, and the streets in the neighbourhood of the Museum were full of open coal-holes, down which sacks were showering; four-wheeled cabs were drawing up and depositing on the pavement corded boxes containing, presumably, the entire wardrobe of some Swiss or Italian family seeking fortune or refuge or some other desirable commodity which is to be found in the boarding-houses of Bloomsbury in the winter. The usual hoarse-voiced men paraded the streets with plants on barrows. Some shouted; others sang. London was like a workshop. London was like a machine. We were all being shot backwards and forwards on this plain foundation to make some pattern. The British Museum was another department of the factory. The swing-doors swung open; and there one stood under the vast dome, as if one were a thought in the huge bald forehead which is so splendidly encircled by a band of famous names. One went to the counter; one took a slip of paper; one opened a volume of the catalogue, and . . . . . the five dots here indicate five separate minutes of stupefaction, wonder and bewilderment. Have you any notion of how many books are written about women in the course of one year? Have you any notion how many are written by men? Are you aware that you are, perhaps, the most discussed animal in the universe? Here had I come with a notebook and a pencil proposing to spend a morning reading, supposing that at the end of the morning I should have transferred the truth to my notebook. But I should need to be a herd of elephants, I thought, and a wilderness of spiders, desperately referring to the animals that are reputed longest lived and most multitudinously eyed, to cope with all this. I should need claws of steel and beak of brass even to penetrate the husk. How shall I ever find the grains of truth embedded in all this mass of paper? I asked myself, and in despair began running my eye up and down the long list of titles. Even the names of the books gave me food for thought. Sex and its nature might well attract doctors and biologists; but what was surprising and difficult of explanation was the fact that sex – woman, that is to say – also attracts agreeable essayists, light-fingered novelists, young men who have taken the M.A. degree; men who have taken no degree; men who have no apparent qualification save that they are not women. Some of these books were, on the face of it, frivolous and facetious; but many, on the other hand, were serious and prophetic, moral and hortatory. Merely to read the titles suggested innumerable schoolmasters, innumerable clergymen mounting their platforms and pulpits and holding forth with loquacity which far exceeded the hour usually allotted to such discourse on this one subject. It was a most strange phenomenon; and apparently – here I consulted the letter M – one confined to the male sex. Women do not write books about men – a fact that I could not help welcoming with relief, for if I had first to read all that men have written about women, then all that women have written about men, the aloe that flowers once in a hundred years would flower twice before I could set pen to paper. So, making a perfectly arbitrary choice of a dozen volumes or so, I sent my slips of paper to lie in the wire tray, and waited in my stall, among the other seekers for the essential oil of truth.

What could be the reason, then, of this curious disparity, I wondered, drawing cart-wheels on the slips of paper provided by the

British taxpayer for other purposes. Why are women, judging from this catalogue, so much more interesting to men than men are to women? A very curious fact it seemed, and my mind wandered to picture the lives of men who spend their time in writing books about women; whether they were old or young, married or unmarried, red-nosed or hump-backed – anyhow, it was flattering, vaguely, to feel oneself the object of such attention, provided that it was not entirely bestowed by the crippled and the infirm – so I pondered until all such frivolous thoughts were ended by an avalanche of books sliding down on to the desk in front of me. Now the trouble began.

FRANCES HOROVITZ
(1938–83)

Romeo and Juliet at the Old Vic

A clear flame
now still
now trembling
on the empty stage

Desire remote to us
thirteen year olds
from shabby Walthamstow
tittering in the balcony.
I, fierce, hissing in the dark
'*Shut up, you fools*'
yearned through shafts of light
to that white face
that fluting bird's voice
passion snared

Tearless, rapt
with secret flowering grief
I stumbled down stone steps
vowed to beauty & to love

Death? We knew
the mimic lovers rose again.
The long and little deaths of love
we could not know,
not Juliet, nor us
nor that young actress
famous now,
ageing, twice divorced
burning still
beyond her brilliant masks

JOHN GREENING
(b. 1954)

At Tate Modern
for John Haines

A glass of our tea-coloured
Thames will gaze as clear
as a Mayan crystal skull
if left to stand. At last,

these few tidal moments
in the Tate, drinking sweet
talk of Edwin Muir,
George Mackay Brown,

Donne encrypted on the north
bank, wrapped in his shroud,
a proud dome resisting
the Blitz. I imagine you

beyond this shaky Millennium
Bridge, beyond the Sound
of Chief Seattle, beyond
the tittle-tattle Interstate,

swaddled against consuming
blizzards, tracking the metaphysical, freeing wilderness
from its trap, knowing a man

must sometimes be an island.

THOMAS HARDY
(1840–1928)

In the British Museum

'What do you see in that time-touched stone,
  When nothing is there
But ashen blankness, although you give it
  A rigid stare?

'You look not quite as if you saw,
  But as if you heard,
Parting your lips, and treading softly
  As mouse or bird.

'It is only the base of a pillar, they'll tell you,
  That came to us
From a far old hill men used to name
  Areopagus.'

– 'I know no art, and I only view
  A stone from a wall,
But I am thinking that stone has echoed
  The voice of Paul;

'Paul as he stood and preached beside it
  Facing the crowd,
A small gaunt figure with wasted features,
  Calling out loud

'Words that in all their intimate accents
  Pattered upon
That marble front, and were wide reflected,
  And then were gone.

'I'm a labouring man, and know but little,
  Or nothing at all;
But I can't help thinking that stone once echoed
  The voice of Paul.'

9

THE COUNTRYMAN IN TOWN

. . . then he repents his wanderings & eyes
The distant forest.

William Blake, *Jerusalem*

WILLIAM WORDSWORTH
(1770–1850)

from *The Prelude*

As the black storm upon the mountain top
Sets off the sunbeam in the valley, so
That huge fermenting mass of humankind
Serves as a solemn background, or relief,
To single forms and objects, whence they draw,
For feeling and contemplative regard,
More than inherent liveliness and power.
How oft, amid those overflowing streets,
Have I gone forward with the crowd, and said
Unto myself, 'The face of every one
That passes by me is a mystery!'
Thus have I looked, nor ceased to look, oppressed
By thoughts of what and whither, when and how,
Until the shapes before my eyes became
A second-sight procession, such as glides
Over still mountains, or appears in dreams;
And once, far-travelled in such mood, beyond
The reach of common indication, lost
Amid the moving pageant, I was smitten
Abruptly, with the view (a sight not rare)
Of a blind Beggar, who, with upright face,
Stood, propped against a wall, upon his chest
Wearing a written paper, to explain
His story, whence he came, and who he was.
Caught by the spectacle my mind turned round
As with the might of waters; an apt type
This label seemed of the utmost we can know,
Both of ourselves and of the universe;
And, on the shape of that unmoving man,
His steadfast face and sightless eyes, I gazed,
As if admonished from another world.

JOHN CLARE
(1793–1864)

This is London!

'This is London!' I exclaimed he laughed at my ignorance & only increased my wonder by saying we were yet several miles from it on the night that we got into London it was announced in the play Bills that a song of mine was to be sung at Covent Garden by Madame Vestris & we was to have gone but it was too late I felt uncommonly pleased at the circumstance we took a walk in the town by moonlight & went to Westminster bridge to see the River Thames I had heard large wonders about its width of water but I was dissapointed thinking I should have seen a freshwater sea when I saw it was less in my eye than Whittlesea Meer I was uncommonly astonished to see so many ladys as I thought them walking about the streets I expressd my surprise & was told they were girls of the town as a modest woman rarely venturd out by herself at nightfall the next morning everything was so uncommon to what I had been used to that the excess of novelty confounded my instinct everything hung round my confused imagination like riddles unsolved while I was there I rarely knew what I was seeing & when I got home my remembrance of objects seemed in a mass one mingled in another like the mosaic squares in a Roman pavement

I had often heard of the worlds seven wonders in my reading days at school but I found in London alone thousands Octave took me to see most of the curiositys we went to Westminster abbey to see the poets corner & to both Playhouses were I saw Kean & Macready & Knight & Munden & Emery the two latter pleased me most of all but the plays were bad ones Burkhardt took me to Vauxhall & made me shut my eyes till I got in the midst of the place & when I opened them I almost fancyd myself in a faireyland but the repetition of the roundabout walk put the Romance out of my head & made it faded reality – these were the scenes that he delighted in & he wishd to take me sometime to see the Beggers Opera a public house so calld the resort of [ ] but we had no time I had had a romantic sort of notion about authors & had an anxious desire to see them fancying they were beings different to other men but the spell was soon broken when I became acquainted with them but I did not see many save at Taylors Dinner partys were Charles

124

Lamb & young Reynolds & Allan Cunningham & Cary with Wainewright the painter often met.

★ ★ ★

When I used to go anywhere by myself especially Mrs. E's I used to sit at night till very late because I was loath to start not for the sake of leaving the company but for fear of meeting with supernatural [agents] even in the busy paths of London though I was a stubborn disbeliever of such things in the daytime yet at night their terrors came upon me tenfold & my head was as full of the terrible as a gossip's thin death-like shadows & goblins with saucer eyes were continually shaping on the darkness from my haunted imagination & when I saw anyone of a spare figure in the dark passing or going on by my side my blood has curdled cold at the foolish apprehensions of his being a supernatural agent whose errand might be to carry me away at the first dark alley we came to

I saw Hazlitt & from him I had learned some fearful disclosures of the place he used to caution me if ever I happend to go to be on my guard as if I once lost my way I shoud sure lose my life as the street Ladys would inveigle me into a fine house were I shoud never be seen agen & he describd the pathways on the street as full of trapdoors which dropd down as soon as pressd on with the feet & sprung in their places after the unfortunate countryman had fallen into the deep hole as if nothing had been were he woud be robd & murderd & thrown into boiling cauldrons kept continually boiling for that purpose & his bones sold to the doctors – with these terrible jealousys in my apprehension I kept a continual lookout & fancied every lady I met a decoyer & every gentleman a pickpocket & if they did but offer any civility my suspicions were confirmd at once & I felt often when walking behind Gilchrist almost fit to take hold of his coat laps

★ ★ ★

I could not bear to go down the dark narrow street of Chancery Lane It was as bad as a haunted place to pass & one dark night I decided to venture the risk of being lost rather than go down though I tried all my courage to go down to no purpose for I could not get it out of my head but that I should be sure to meet death or the devil if I did so I passed it & tried to find Fleet Street by another road but I soon got lost & the more I tried to find the way the more I got wrong so I offered a watchman a shilling to show me the way thither but he said he would not go for that & asked a half-a-crown which I readily gave him

The Melancholy Death of Lord Byron

When I was in London the melancholy death of Lord Byron was announced in the public papers & I saw his remains borne away out of the city on its last journey to that place where fame never comes His funeral was blazed in the papers with the usual parade that accompanies the death of great men I happened to see it by chance as I was wandering up Oxford Street on my way to Mrs Emmerson's when my eye was suddenly arrested by straggling groups of the common people collected together & talking about a funeral I did as the rest did though I could not get hold of what funeral it could be but I knew it was not a common one by the curiosity that kept watch on every countenance By & by the group collected into about a hundred or more when the train of a funeral suddenly appeared on which a young girl that stood beside me gave a deep sigh & uttered 'Poor Lord Byron' I looked up at the young girl's face it was dark & beautiful & I could almost feel in love with her for the sigh she had uttered for the poet it was worth all the newspaper puffs & magazine mournings that ever were paraded after the death of a poet The common people felt his merits & his power & the common people of a country are the best feelings of a prophecy of futurity they are the veins & arteries that feed & quicken the heart of living fame The breathings of eternity & the soul of time are indicated in that prophecy They felt by a natural impulse that the mighty was fallen & they moved in saddened silence the streets were lined on each side as the procession passed but they were all the commonest of the lower orders the young girl that stood by me had counted the carriages in her mind as they passed & she told me there were sixty three or four in all they were of all sorts & sizes & made up a motley show the gilt ones that led the procession were empty the hearse looked small & rather mean & the coach that followed carried his embers in an urn over which a pall was thrown I believe that his liberal principles in religion & politics did a great deal towards gaining the notice & affections of the lower orders Be as it will it is better to be beloved by those low & humble for undisguised honesty than flattered by the great for purchased & pensioned hypocrisies

from *Autobiography*

TED HUGHES
(1930–98)

Epiphany

London. The grimy lilac softness
Of an April evening. Me
Walking over Chalk Farm Bridge
On my way to the tube station.
A new father – slightly light-headed
With the lack of sleep and the novelty.
Next, this young fellow coming towards me.

I glanced at him for the first time as I passed him
Because I noticed (I couldn't believe it)
What I'd been ignoring.

Not the bulge of a small animal
Buttoned into the top of his jacket
The way colliers used to wear their whippets –
But its actual face. Eyes reaching out
Trying to catch my eyes – so familiar!
The huge ears, the pinched, urchin expression –
The wild confronting stare, pushed through fear,
Between the jacket lapels.
                                    'It's a fox-cub!'
I heard my own surprise as I stopped.
He stopped. 'Where did you get it? What
Are you going to do with it?'
                                    A fox-cub
On the hump of Chalk Farm Bridge!

'You can have him for a pound.' 'But
Where did you find it? What will you do with it?'
'Oh, somebody'll buy him. Cheap enough
At a pound.' And a grin.
                                    What I was thinking
Was – what would you think? How would we fit it

Into our crate of space? With the baby?
What would you make of its old smell
And its mannerless energy?
And as it grew up and began to enjoy itself
What would we do with an unpredictable,
Powerful, bounding fox?
The long-mouthed, flashing temperament?
That necessary nightly twenty miles
And that vast hunger for everything beyond us?
How would we cope with its cosmic derangements
Whenever we moved?

The little fox peered past me at other folks,
At this one and at that one, then at me.
Good luck was all it needed.
Already past the kittenish
But the eyes still small,
Round, orphaned-looking, woebegone
As if with weeping. Bereft
Of the blue milk, the toys of feather and fur,
The den life's happy dark. And the huge whisper
Of the constellations
Out of which Mother had always returned.
My thoughts felt like big, ignorant hounds
Circling and sniffing around him.
                              Then I walked on
As if out of my own life.
I let that fox-cub go. I tossed it back
Into the future
Of a fox-cub in London and I hurried
Straight on and dived as if escaping
Into the Underground. If I had paid,
If I had paid that pound and turned back
To you, with that armful of fox –

If I had grasped that whatever comes with a fox
Is what tests a marriage and proves it a marriage –
I would not have failed the test. Would you have failed it?
But I failed. Our marriage had failed.

GRACE NICHOLS
(b. 1950)

Island Man

(for a Caribbean island man in London who still wakes up to the sound of the sea)

Morning
and island man wakes up
to the sound of blue surf
in his head
the steady breaking and wombing

wild seabirds
and fishermen pushing out to sea
the sun surfacing defiantly

from the east
of his small emerald island
he always comes back   groggily groggily

Comes back to sands
of a grey metallic soar
                              to surge of wheels
in dull North Circular roar

muffling muffling
his crumpled pillow waves
island man heaves himself

Another London day

THOMAS HARDY
(1840–1928)

To a Tree in London

(CLEMENT'S INN)

Here you stay
Night and day
Never, never going away!

Do you ache
When we take
Holiday for our health's sake?

Wish for feet
When the heat
Scalds you in the brick-built street,

That you might
Climb the height
Where your ancestry saw light,

Find a brook
In some nook
There to purge your swarthy look?

No. You read
Trees to need
Smoke like earth whereon to feed . . .

Have no sense
That far hence
Air is sweet in a blue immense

Thus, black, blind,
You have opined
Nothing of your brightest kind;

Never seen
Miles of green
Smelt the landscape's sweet serene.

Lucy's Letter

Things harness me here. I long
for we labrish bad. Doors
not fixed open here.
No Leela either. No cousin
Lil, Miss Lottie or Bro'-Uncle.
Dayclean doesn't have cockcrowin'.
Midmornin' doesn' bring
Cousin-Maa with her naseberry tray.
Afternoon doesn' give a ragged
Manwell, strung with fish
like bright leaves. Seven days
play same note in London, chile.
But Leela, money-rustle regular.

Mi dear, I don' laugh now,
not'n' like we thunder claps
in darkness on verandah.
I turned a battery hen
in 'lectric light, day an' night.
No mood can touch one
mango season back at Yard.
At least though I did start
evening school once.
An' doctors free, chile.

London isn't like we
village dirt road, you know
Leela: it a parish
of a pasture-lan' what
grown crisscross streets,
an' they lie down to my door.
But I lock myself in.
I carry keys everywhere.
Life here's no open summer,

girl. But Sat'day mornin' don'
find mi han' dry, don' find mi face
a heavy cloud over the man.

An' though he still have
a weekend mind for bat 'n' ball
he wash a dirty dish now, mi dear.
It sweet him I on the Pill.

We get money for holidays.
But there's no sun-hot
to enjoy cool breeze.

Leela, I really a sponge
you know, for traffic noise,
for work noise, for halfway
intentions, for halfway smiles,
for clockwatchin' an' col' weather.
I hope you don' think I gone
too fat when we meet.
I booked up to come an' soak
the children in daylight.

---

labrish: to talk and gossip without restraint
naseberry tray: seller's tray of naseberries: roughish brown, soft and sweet,
Caribbean fruit about the size of a small apple.

WILLIAM WORDSWORTH
(1770–1850)

The Reverie of Poor Susan

At the corner of Wood Street, when daylight appears,
Hangs a Thrush that sings loud, it has sung for three years:
Poor Susan has passed by the spot, and has heard
In the silence of morning the song of the bird.

'Tis a note of enchantment; what ails her? She sees
A mountain ascending, a vision of trees;
Bright volumes of vapour through Lothbury glide.
And a river flows on through the vale of Cheapside.

Green pastures she views in the midst of the dale
Down which she so often has tripp'd with her pail;
And a single small cottage, a nest like a dove's,
The one only dwelling on earth that she loves.

She looks, and her heart is in heaven: but they fade,
The mist and the river, the hill and the shade;
The stream will not flow, and the hill will not rise,
And the colours have all pass'd away from her eyes!

10

THE RECENT WARS

Across Europe, across Africa, in howling & deadly War.
A sheet & veil & curtain of blood is let down from Heaven

★   ★   ★

Jerusalem's Pillars fall in the rendings of fierce War
Over France & Germany, upon the Rhine & Danube.
Reuben & Benjamin flee: they hide in the Valley of Rephaim.

William Blake, *Jerusalem*

RUDYARD KIPLING

(1865–1936)

London Stone
(Nov. 11, 1923)

When you come to London Town,
    (Grieving – grieving!)
Bring your flowers and lay them down
    At the place of grieving.

When you come to London Town,
    (Grieving – grieving!)
Bow your head and mourn your own,
    With the others grieving.

For those minutes, let it wake
    (Grieving – grieving!)
All the empty-heart and ache
    That is not cured by grieving.

For those minutes, tell no lie:
    (Grieving – grieving!)
'Grave, this is thy victory;
    And the sting of death is grieving.'

Where's our help, from Earth or Heaven
    (Grieving – grieving!)
To comfort us for what we've given,
    And only gained the grieving?

Heaven's too far and Earth too near,
    (Grieving – grieving!)
But our neighbour's standing here,
    Grieving as we're grieving.

What's his burden every day?
    (Grieving – grieving!)
Nothing man can count or weigh,
    But loss and love's own grieving.

What is the tie betwixt us two
   (Grieving – grieving!)
That must last our whole lives through?
   'As I suffer, so do you.'
That may ease the grieving.

STEVIE SMITH
(1903–71)

A Soldier Dear to Us

It was the War
I was a child
They came from the trenches
To our suburb mild.

Our suburb then was more a country place
They came to our house for release.

In the convalescent Army hospital
That was once a great house and landed estate
Lay Basil, wounded on the Somme,
But his pain was not now so great

That he could not be fetched in a bath-chair
Or hobble on crutches to find in our house there
My mother and aunt, his friends on leave, myself (I was
    twelve)
And a hearth rug to lie down in front of the fire on and rest
    himself.

It was a November golden and wet
As there had been little wind that year and the leaves were yet
Yellow on the great trees, on the oak trees and elms
Of our beautiful suburb, as it was then.

When Basil woke up he liked to talk and laugh
He was a sweet-tempered laughing man, he said:
'My dear, listen to this' then he read
From The Church Times, how angry the Bishop was because
Of the Reserved Sacrament in the church
Of St Alban's, Holborn. 'Now, my dear' he said, 'for a treat
Next Sunday I will take you to All Saints, Margaret Street;
    only
You will have to sit on the ladies' side, though you are not yet
    one really.'

Basil never spoke of the trenches, but I
Saw them always, saw the mud, heard the guns, saw the
   duckboards,
Saw the men and the horses slipping in the great mud, saw
The rain falling and never stop, saw the gaunt
Trees and the rusty frame
Of the abandoned gun carriages. Because it was the same
As the poem 'Childe Roland to the Dark Tower Came'
I was reading at school.

Basil and Tommy and Joey Porteous who came to our house
Were too brave even to ask *themselves* if there was any hope
So I laughed as they laughed, as they laughed when Basil said:
What will Ronny do now (it was Ronny Knox) will he pope?

And later, when he had poped, Tommy gave me his book for
   a present,
'The Spiritual Aeneid' and I read of the great torment
Ronny had had to decide, Which way, this or that?
But I thought Basil and Tommy and Joey Porteous were
   more brave than that.

Coming to our house
Were the brave ones. And I could not look at them
For my strong feelings, except
Slantingly, from the hearth rug, look at them.

Oh Basil, Basil, you had such a merry heart
But you taught me a secret you did not perhaps mean to impart,
That one must speak lightly, and use fair names like the ladies
They used to call
The Eumenides.

Oh Basil
I was a child at school,
My school lessons coloured
My thoughts of you.

Envoi

Tommy and Joey Porteous were killed in France. Now
    fifty years later
Basil has died of the shots he got in the shell crater
The shrapnel has worked round at last to his merry heart,
    I write this
For a memorial of the soldier dear to us he was.

LOUIS MacNEICE
(1907–63)

Troll's Courtship

I am a lonely Troll after my gala night;
I have knocked down houses and stamped my feet on the
    people's heart,
I have trundled round the sky with the executioner's cart
And dropped my bait for corpses, watched them bite,
But I am a lonely Troll – nothing in the end comes right.

In a smoking and tinkling dawn with fires and broken glass
I am a lonely Troll; my tributes are in vain
To Her to whom if I had even a human brain
I might have reached but, as it is, the epochs pass
And leave me unfulfilled, no further than I was.

Because I cannot accurately conceive
Any ideal, even ideal Death,
My curses and my boasts are merely a waste of breath,
My lusts and lonelinesses grunt and heave
And blunder round among the ruins that I leave.

Yet from the lubber depths of my unbeing I
Aspire to Her who was my Final Cause but who
Is always somewhere else and not to be spoken to,
Is always nowhere: which is in the long run why
I make for nowhere, make a shambles of the sky.

Nostalgia for the breasts that never gave nor could
Give milk or even warmth has desolated me,
Clutching at shadows of my nullity
Thant slink and mutter through the leafless wood
Which thanks to me is dead, is dead for good.

A cone of ice enclosing liquid fire,
Utter negation in a positive form,
That would be how She is, the nadir and the norm
Of dissolution and the constant pyre
Of all desirable things – that is what I desire

And therefore cry to Her with the voice of broken bells
To come, visibly, palpably, to come,
Gluing my ear to gutted walls but walls are dumb,
All I can catch is a gurgle as of the sea in shells
But not Her voice – for She is always somewhere else.

May, 1941

STEPHEN SPENDER
(1909–95)

Rejoice in the Abyss

The great pulsation passed. Glass lay around me
Resurrected from the end. I walked
Along streets of slate-jabbering houses,

Against an acrid cloud of dust, I saw
The houses kneel, revealed each in its abject
Prayer, my prayer as well: 'Oh God,
Spare me the lot that is my neighbour's.'

Then, in the upper sky, indifferent to our
Sulphurous nether hell, I saw
The dead of the bombed graveyard, a calm tide
Under the foam of stars above the town.

And on the roof-tops there stood London prophets
Saints of Covent Garden, Parliament Hill Fields,
Hampstead, Hyde Park Corner, Saint John's Wood,
Crying aloud in cockney fanatic voices:
'In the midst of Life is Death!' They kneeled
And prayed against the misery manufactured
In mines and ships and mills, against
The greed of merchants, vanity of priests.
They sang: 'We souls from the abyss
To whom the stars are fields of flowers,
Tell you: Rejoice in the abyss!
For hollow is the skull, the vacuum
In the gold ball, St Paul's gold cross.
Unless you will accept the emptiness
Within the bells of foxgloves and cathedrals,
Each life must feed upon the deaths of others,
The shamelessly entreating prayer
Of every house will be that it is spared
Calamity that strikes its neighbour.'

U. A. FANTHORPE
(b. 1929)

Underground
(Henry Moore's *A Shelter Sketchbook*)

They have come as far as there is,
Under the tree-roots, the sewers,
Under drains, cables, flood-plains.

They sprawl, wrapped in blankets,
Waiting like tubers for spring, the all-clear.
At Belsize Park, Cricklewood,

The Liverpool Street Extension,
Londoners lie under London, incubating
A difficult energy, a different life.

Round the corner the artist watches,
Jotting notes on an envelope.
To have drawn from life would be like

Sketching in the hold of a slave ship.
Not the Cockney wags of legend, but huge
Muffled forms, trussed and bandaged

Like Lazarus. Wood and stone,
As well as bones and veins, wait inside
These vast vulnerabilities.

From their coding, we can construe
Houses falling, bridges falling, London falling,
Civilisations falling down. The artist

Must show this without saying. Just
His sketchbook's sotto-voce: *Abstractish figures shelter background,*
And *Try white again then scramble dryish grey over.*

Also he shows the women knitting,
People holding hands, sleeping,
And thinking. Particularly thinking.

From these rhizomes the future will rise,
Equivocal, chancy. Crowned stones
On a northern moor, too big for houses,

And paper-shrouded Cardboard Citizens,
Sleeping in Strand doorways, neighbours to rubbish,
And all stations between. As Cabot

Aimed for Japan, got Newfoundland instead,
These monstrous eggs may hatch surprisingly.

Above them, paving stones and tarmac sag,
Windows taped into resistance, the hunched
Apprehensive roofs of Cricklewood

And Belsize Park, the Liverpool Street Extension,
Guns, smoke, cloud, fighters, bombers, fire, air,

Under the City, in the sky, pitched
Between heaven and humanity, as we are,
The tube trains shuttling between,

And the artist taking notes round the corner.

RUTH PITTER
(1897–1992)

Musa Translated
(with apologies to William Blake)

There Musa inhabited with horror – there
With River-Foggs and Murkiness and Smuts continual,
Under the unending Downpour of Stygian Coaldust
From Lot's-Road, where if Mrs Lot had been so silly
As to have turn'd into Salt, she would have been blackt-out
In a Night and a Day: where the dismall Fume ariseth
From the Place where they will not stop making the hellish
  Crucibles;
Where Housewives decline the Attempt to keep clean any more,
For (as they mournfully affirm) it's no use busting yourself,
When you've got round the Place once, it's time to start cleaning
  again.
And this Place, by the tortuousness of the Human Genius,
Costs dearly, and is accounted a desirable Neighbourhood.
There liv'd the Cat Musa, enwrapt in her Female Garment,
And there she conceiv'd her young amid demon sexual Howlings
Appropriate to those Bohemian Haunts – far different from the
  gentle
Regenerated Accents, the heavenly Voice of Sublimated Love.
But when to the Charms of the Blessed Region were added
The squalling Alert and the sickening Scream and Whump
Of sacrilegious Projectiles, scathing th' idyllic Cradle
Of so many and various Loves – when Beings with tin Hats
And too many Whiskers stood on the Edges of Craters
Trying to recall if that were the Place where they had once liv'd
  with a Model
For almost three Weeks, and kindly hoping that the Fair One
(If that were the place indeed) had been luckily evicted
For non-payment of Rent, before the hellish Catastrophe –
Then indeed did the Owners of Musa, a worthy Couple
Of the stockbroking Sort, who affected our murky Strand
Out of pure Snobbishness, and Meekness to grown-up Children –
Think of their Cottage in Essex with modest Satisfaction.

And seeing that the fair Musa was great with Young
They popt her into the Car, enclosed in a Basket.
She, vibrant with Rage and Fear, imperative protesting,
Hurling herself with hysterick Leaps against the Enclosure,
Cursing the Universe in general, and more particularly the Cook
    who held her
Until any creature but Cat would have miscarried incontinent,
Was whiz'd through three circles of hell, through Stratford
    Broadway,
Through the Region Elenore via Steeple Bumsted to Stickey End,
And deposited with a Thump on a Kitchen Table;
While the Demon Cook, muttering dark venoms, rusht for the
    Primus,
Because that is the quickest Thing in the World to boil a Kettle,
Except bone-dry dead Twiggs, which she did not know about,
And if she had known would have condemn'd with Revilings
Since the whole Pride of the Craft revolts against pitiful Doings,
And aught uncostly, not bought or sold, they condemn as pitiful.

LOUIS MacNEICE
(1907–63)

The Streets of Laredo

O early one morning I walked out like Agag,
Early one morning to walk through the fire
Dodging the pythons that leaked on the pavements
With tinkle of glasses and tangle of wire;

When grimed to the eyebrows I met an old fireman
Who looked at me wryly and thus did he say:
'The streets of Laredo are closed to all traffic,
We won't never master this joker to-day.

'O hold the branch tightly and wield the axe brightly,
The bank is in powder, the banker's in hell,
But loot is still free on the streets of Laredo
And when we drive home we drive home on the bell.'

Then out from a doorway there sidled a cockney,
A rocking-chair rocking on top of his head:
'O fifty-five years I been feathering my love-nest
And look at it now – why, you'd sooner be dead.'

At which there arose from a wound in the asphalt,
His big wig a-smoulder, Sir Christopher Wren
Saying: 'Let them make hay of the streets of Laredo;
When your ground-rents expire I will build them again.'

Then twangling their bibles with wrath in their nostrils
From Bonehill Fields came Bunyan and Blake:
'Laredo the golden is fallen, is fallen;
Your flame shall not quench nor your thirst shall not slake.'

'I come to Laredo to find me asylum',
Says Tom Dick and Harry the Wandering Jew;
'They tell me report at the first police station
But the station is pancaked – so what can I do?'

Thus eavesdropping sadly I strolled through Laredo
Perplexed by the dicta misfortunes inspire
Till one low last whisper inveigled my earhole –
The voice of the Angel, the voice of the fire:

O late, very late, have I come to Laredo
A whimsical bride in my new scarlet dress
But at last I took pity on those who were waiting
To see my regalia and feel my caress.

No ring the bells gaily and play the hose daily,
Put splints on your legs, put a gag on your breath;
O you streets of Laredo, you streets of Laredo,
Lay down the red carpet – My dowry is death.

July, 1945

11

SUBURBS, PARKS AND GARDENS

Immediately the Lark mounted with a loud trill from Felpham's
  Vale,
And the Wild Thyme from Wimbleton's green & impurpled
  Hills.
And Los & Enitharmon rose over the Hills of Surrey

William Blake, *Milton*, book 2

STEVIE SMITH
(1903–71)

Avondale

How sweet the birds of Avondale
Of Avondale, of Avondale,
How sweet the birds of Avondale
Do swoop and swing and call.

The children too of Avondale,
Of Avondale, of Avondale,
The boys and girls of Avondale
Do swoop and swing and call,

And all the little cats and dogs,
Of Avondale, of Avondale,
In their own way in Avondale
Do swoop and swing and call,

And oh it is a pleasant sight
It is a very pleasant sight
To see the creatures so delight
To swoop and swing and call,
In Avondale, in Avondale,
To see them swoop and call.

JOHN GREENING
(b. 1954)

Kew

What am I trying to
get into with this one
old penny?
       the turnstile
clicks satisfyingly
its glossy black coldness
lets me through

       the turnstile
moves just one way, admits
only one memory
at a time
       the turnstile
opens its prison bars
on to my first year at
Kew Gardens
       the turnstile
still turns, my penny rests
on that eye of the dead.

There is no queue. To leave
it costs nothing. Just push
the turnstile

       you are tired
but though your legs won't work
no pushchair can pass through
the turnstile
       this Easter
we have been revived by
what can be seen beyond
the turnstile
       but where is
Grandpa? Where is Auntie
Daisy? Haven't I grown . . .

the turnstile
groans its own reply. No
Admittance After Dusk.

ANNE STEVENSON
(b. 1933)

'All Canal Boat Cruises Start Here'

(Regent's Park, 1987)

A musk of kittening
snuffed out her morning dream:
the childhood tabby whelping on her mother's shoes.
Still no one could find those
x-ray photographs of embryos.

'I didn't know I could dream smells,'
she said at breakfast.
'You're pregnant,' he said. 'You're a miracle.'
'I'm guilty where there's too much evil.'

Later they walked by the canal:
the Sunday crush, the peacefulness,
a crowd of sleepy explosives spoiling the waterfowl,
exclusive wagging dogs, the lovers' binary excuse,
the straggling families.

'They don't see us,
they're all wound up in themselves,' as she
looked understanding at one impervious mamma,
the daughter's pale silk hair shining,
a sulky boy scuffing behind.

Was that it? That look flashing (was he?)
furtive, from a second-hand suit?
Scary, the shabby solitary, hating you
and apologizing.

In the fenced off zoo, an elephant
took a tiny white keeper for a trot.
And, crikey! that barge cat
leaping three feet of slime to the quay.

But in painful labour
it was blue sky and fishermen she remembered,
each hopeful alone
in his nest of a basket and stool.

'They didn't catch fish,
but love, what a guard of honour,'
as the waving drawbridge of rods
bowed the pleasure boats through.

JOHN KEATS
(1795–1821)

To a Nightingale

My heart aches, and a drowsy numbness pains
   My sense, as though of hemlock I had drunk,
Or emptied some dull opiate to the drains
   One minute past, and Lethe-wards had sunk:
'Tis not through envy of thy happy lot,
   But being too happy in thy happiness, –
      That thou, light-winged Dryad of the trees,
        In some melodious plot
   Of beechen green, and shadows numberless,
     Singest of summer in full-throated ease.

O for a draught of vintage, that hath been
   Cool'd a long age in the deep-delved earth,
Tasting of Flora and the country-green,
   Dance, and Provençal song, and sun-burnt mirth!
O for a beaker full of the warm South,
   Full of the true, the blushful Hippocrene,
      With beaded bubbles winking at the brim,
        And purple-stained mouth;
   That I might drink and leave the world unseen
     And with thee fade away into the forest dim:

Fade far away, dissolve, and quite forget
   What thou among the leaves hast never known,
The weariness, the fever, and the fret
   Here, where men sit and hear each other groan;
Where palsy shakes a few, sad, last grey hairs,
   Where youth grows pale, and spectre-thin, and dies;
      Where but to think is to be full of sorrow
        And leaden-eyed despairs;
   Where beauty cannot keep her lustrous eyes,
     Or new Love pine at them beyond to-morrow.

Away! away! for I will fly to thee,
  Not charioted by Bacchus and his pards,
But on the viewless wings of Poesy,
  Though the dull brain perplexes and retards:
Already with thee! tender is the night,
    And haply the Queen-Moon is on her throne,
      Cluster'd around by all her starry Fays;
        But here there is no light,
    Save what from heaven is with the breezes blown
      Through verdurous glooms and winding mossy ways.

I cannot see what flowers are at my feet,
  Nor what soft incense hangs upon the boughs,
But, in embalmed darkness, guess each sweet
  Wherewith the seasonable month endows
The grass, the thicket, and the fruit-tree wild;
    White hawthorn, and the pastoral eglantine;
      Fast-fading violets cover'd up in leaves;
        And mid-May's eldest child,
    The coming musk-rose, full of dewy wine,
      The murmurous haunt of flies on summer eves.

Darkling I listen; and for many a time
  I have been half in love with easeful Death,
Call'd him soft names in many a mused rhyme,
  To take into the air my quiet breath;
Now more than ever seems it rich to die,
    To cease upon the midnight with no pain,
      While thou art pouring forth thy soul abroad
        In such an ecstasy!
    Still wouldst thou sing, and I have ears in vain –
      To thy high requiem become a sod.

Thou wast not born for death, immortal Bird!
   No hungry generations tread thee down;
The voice I hear this passing night was heard
   In ancient days by emperor and clown:
Perhaps the self-same song that found a path
    Through the sad heart of Ruth, when sick for home,
      She stood in tears amid the alien corn;
        The same that oft-times hath
    Charm'd magic casements, opening on the foam
      Of perilous seas, in faery lands forlorn.

Forlorn! the very word is like a bell
   To toll me back from thee to my sole self.
Adieu! the fancy cannot cheat so well
   As she is famed to do, deceiving elf,
Adieu! adieu! thy plaintive anthem fades
    Past the near meadows, over the still stream,
      Up the hill-side; and now 'tis buried deep
        In the next valley-glades:
    Was it a vision, or a waking dream?
      Fled is that music:– do I wake or sleep?

JOHN CLARE
(1793–1864)

from *Natural History Letters (1825–37)*

Helpstone

I forgot to say in my last that the Nightingale sung as common by day
as night & as often tho its a fact that is not generaly known your
Londoners are very fond of talking about the bird & I believe fancy
every bird they hear after sunset a Nightingale I remember while I was
there last while walking with a friend in the fields of Shacklwell we
saw a gentleman & lady listening very attentive by the side of a shrub-
bery & when we came up we heard them lavishing praises on the beautiful song of the nightingale which happend to be a thrush but it did
for them & they listend & repeated their praise with heartfelt satisfaction while the bird seemed to know the grand distinction that its song
had gaind for it & strove exultingly to keep up the deception by
attempting a varied & more louder song the dews was ready to fall but
the lady was heedless of the wet grass tho the setting sun as a traveller
glad to rest was leaning his enlarged rim on the earth like a table of fire
& lessening by degrees out of sight leaving night & a few gilt clouds
behind him such is the ignorance of Nature in large Citys that are
nothing less than overgrown prisons that shut out the world and all its
beautys

JOHN HEATH-STUBBS
(b. 1918)

London Magpie

Magpie, it's great to hear your chuckle
Among the streets and squares of my part of London,
Though you're bad news, I fear,
For the little singing birds I love so well,
Who are trying to rear their broods now, in treacherous April;
You and your flash brother
The jay, and your dingy cousin the carrion crow –
Egg thieves and baby-snatchers
All of you, corvid spivs.

PETER PHILLIPS
(b. 1948)

London Cousins

Sometimes I worry about Hampstead;
streets peppered with restaurants,
boutiques fighting for frontage.

Camden looks shiftily over his shoulder,
still the scruffy hooligan;
gets togged up at week-ends.

St John's Wood thinks she's Beverly Hills,
sways her hips, wears
designer burglar alarms.

Kilburn sprawls his lanky High Road,
has a tendency to oversleep,
turns his back on Maida Vale;
she's a social climber –
sexpot made good.

Swiss Cottage is a bit mixed up,
feels anxious, and Finchley
(a second cousin) is doing better;
Waitrose has opened,
there's a Warner Cinema.

I begin to understand
why cousins grow apart.

BENJAMIN ZEPHANIAH
(b. 1958)

Neighbours

I am the type you are supposed to fear
Black and foreign
Big and dreadlocks
An uneducated grass eater.

I talk in tongues
I chant at night
I appear anywhere,
I sleep with lions
And when the moon gets me
I am a Wailer.

I am moving in
Next door to you
So you can get to know me,
You will see my shadow
In the bathroom window,
My aromas will occupy
Your space,
Our ball will be in your court.
How will you feel?

You should feel good
You have been chosen.

I am the type you are supposed to love
Dark and mysterious
Tall and natural
Thinking, tea total.
I talk in schools
I sing on TV
I am in the papers,
I keep cool cats

And when the sun is shining
I go Carnival.

JOHN HEATH-STUBBS
(b.1918)

The Philosophers and the Pomes

A light Augustan breeze
Riffled through the leaves of an apple-tree
In a walled garden at Kensington
(A village not far from London). Isaac Newton
Sat in the latish summer sun. Diamond his dog
Was at his feet and snapped at flies. An apple,
As if already it had intimated
The coming on of autumn and of winter,
Quietly disengaged itself,
Leaving the bough it was suspended from. It fell,
Plummeting towards the centre of the earth,
As though filled with desire. Or was it not
Blind attractive force that drew it,
Just as the magnet rules the iron filings?

Newton observed. Out of his pocket
He took a small and tightly stoppered ink-horn.
Quills and paper were quickly brought to him.
Those quills of the wild goose
Began to scratch and scrawl, to scrawl and scratch,
Through days and months and years. The symbols
Crawled like ants upon the quires, until at length
The trumpet sounded, and the angels fell.
Unsinging now, the heavenly bodies
Whirled and twirled around through empty space
In a beautiful, just, intelligible order.

JAMES HARPUR
(b. 1956)

My Father's Flat

Tugging apart the curtains every day
He always saw, three storeys up, a grand
Sweep of the Thames, the trees of Battersea

And, squatting there, the Japanese pagoda –
Inflaming, a parody of a grandstand,
Its four sides flaunting a golden Buddha.

It glowed like a lantern near the glitzy braid
Of Albert Bridge at night.
                              If he had crossed
The river he might have heard *Renounce the world*

Escape the gilded lips or seen Gautama lying
In mortal sleep, his face relaxed, his flesh released;
Even in death, teaching the art of dying.

At night, across the river two golden eyes burn
Into the heavy velvet of the curtain.

THOMAS HARDY
(1840)

Beyond the Last Lamp

(near Tooting Common)

I

While rain, with eve in partnership,
Descended darkly, drip, drip, drip,
Beyond the last lone lamp I passed
 Walking slowly, whispering sadly,
 Two linked loiterers, wan, downcast:
Some heavy thought constrained each face,
And blinded them to time and place.

II

The pair seemed lovers, yet absorbed
In mental scenes no longer orbed
By love's young rays. Each countenance
 As it slowly, as it sadly
 Caught the lamplight's yellow glance,
Held in suspense a misery
At things which had been or might be.

III

When I retrod that watery way
Some hours beyond the droop of day,
Still I found pacing there the twain
 Just as slowly, just as sadly,
 Heedless of the night and rain.
One could but wonder who they were
And what wild woe detained them there.

IV

Though thirty years of blur and blot
Have slid since I beheld that spot,
And saw in curious converse there
   Moving slowly, moving sadly
   That mysterious tragic pair,
Its olden look may linger on –
All but the couple; they have gone.

V

Whither? Who knows, indeed . . . And yet
To me, when nights are weird and wet,
Without those comrades there at tryst
   Creeping slowly, creeping sadly,
   That lone lane does not exist.
There they seem brooding on their pain,
And will, while such a lane remain.

JON SILKIN
(1930–97)

Urban Grasses

With a sickle, I tended the dead in London
shortening the grass that had flowered
on their bodies, as it had in my child's.
And I piled the soil over the paupers' flesh
in their flimsy coffins, which split. What else
was I to do? It became
My trade, my living.

★   ★   ★

Earth, I shall be unhappy to not know
how you go on, when I'm like those
I tended, shearing the grasses
above their foreheads. I felt tenderness
yet I did not know them – and how should I re-assure
that nothing, and say, yes, I care for you
because you are nothing now. Yet you are nothing.
Could I have dared tell them?
and therefore I remained silent.

12

LONDON TRANSPORT

The Chariot Wheels filled with Eyes rage along the howling
  Valley –

William Blake, Jerusalem

D. J. ENRIGHT
(b. 1920)

The Stations of King's Cross

He is seized and bound by the turnstile.

The moving stair writes once, and having writ,
Moves on.

At Hammersmith the nails
At Green Park the tree.

A despatch case which is well named
A square basket made of rattan
Which is a scourge.
The heel of the Serpent bruises Man's instep.

At Earl's Court a Chopper
New, flashing, spotless
It carries hooks and claws and edges
Which wound.

It is hot. Vee
Wipes her face. Cheek to jowl
She wipes the man's on either side

Rather bear those pills I have
Than fly to others that I know not of.

He speaks to the maidenforms of Jerusalem
Blessed are the paps which never gave suck.

The agony in Covent Garden
He finds them sleeping, for their eyes are heavy.

The first fall, the second fall
The third fall.
And more to come.

171

A sleeve goes, a leg is torn
A hem is ripped.
This is the parting of garments.

They mock him, offering him vodka.
The effect is shattering.

He is taken down from the strap.
And deposited.

Wilt thou leave him in the loathsome grave?

DAVID CONSTANTINE
(b. 1944)

The Forest

Pity about the forest gone up in smoke
And what comes out of it will surely die.
Not just the meat, also the funny folk:
The sow, the goat with faces haunted by
Humanity, the cross-betweens we give
A quid to goggle at, they never live.

Was on the tube once years ago in June
Late, on the wrong line, sleeping, very tight.
Opened an eye at let's say Bethnal Green
And slept again, thinking this can't be right,
And somewhere later, let's say Leytonstone,
Opened the other and a man got on

Naked as Adam, with a donkey's head,
And sat twiddling his ticket. Woke again
Somewhere, I don't know where, the place was dead,
I heard that wind come down the tunnels, then
Girl's steps running and the girl who ran
Got in and sat beside the donkey-man.

They filled my eyes, and when I heard the din
Of our wheels enlarge and we hit fresh air
And were into fields, outside, and blossom blew in
And touched his limbs, her dress, their heads of hair,
I felt we were a well of happiness
Struck luckily and coming up to bless

Mankind. They stood to leave, he steadied her
Against the fall, I saw how bare he was
Below the nape and how the head he bore
Flowered from a spine like mine, how courteous
And solemn his attentions were and what
A pride he showed, handing her down. I sat

Like some forgotten dosser in a pew,
The doors wide open, scents, a hubbub or
Music, a river noise – I knew
It was the forest they were heading for.
My ticket was wrong. I let the damned train start
Back for the city, back to its knotted heart.

CAROLE SATYAMURTI

Ghost Stations

We are the inheritors. We hide here
at the roots of the perverted city
waiting, practising the Pure Way.
Listening to ourselves, each other,
we find the old soiled words won't do;
often we can only dance our meanings.

Deep in the arteries of London, life
is possible − in the forgotten stations:
York Road, St Mary's, Seething Lane . . .
I love the names. Each day, we sing them
like a psalm, a celebration
− Down Street, British Museum, City Road.

We live on waste. After the current's off
we run along tunnels, through sleeping trains,
ahead of the night cleaners. We find chips,
apple cores (the most nutritious part),
dregs of Coke. On good days, we pick up
coins that fit the chocolate machines.

Once I found a whole bag of shopping.
That night we had an iceberg lettuce,
a honeydew melon, tasting of laughter.
And once, an abutilon − its orange
bee-flowers gladdened us for weeks.
Such things are dangerous;

now, to remind ourselves, we read
the newspapers we use as mattresses.
Or gather on the platforms,
witness the trains as they rip past
(our eyes have grown used to the speed).
Almost every known depravity

is acted out on trains – rape, drunkenness,
robbery, fighting, harassment, abuse.
And the subtler forms – intellectual bullying,
contempt, all the varieties of indifference . . .
We've learned to read the faces;
we need to see these things, simply.

The travellers only see their own reflections.
But lately, a few in such despair
they cup their faces to the glass, weeping,
have seen the ghost stations
and though we're always out of sight,
they sense our difference and find their way.

Our numbers are growing, though there are
reverses. Some lose heart, want to leave.
We can't let them – we keep them all
at Brompton Road, carefully guarded,
plotting uselessly, swapping fantasies,
raving of sunlight, mountains or the sea.

One day, we'll climb out, convert the city!
The trains are full of terrible energy;
we only have example, words. But, there is
our chant to strengthen us, our hope-names:
Uxbridge Road, King William Street,
South Kentish Town, South Acton, Bull and Bush . . .

JOHN KEATS
(1795–1821)

from *The Cap and Bells*

The slave retreated backwards, humble-eyed,
And with a slave-like silence closed the door,
And to old Hum thro' street and alley hied;
He 'knew the city,' as we say, of yore,
And for short cuts and turns, was nobody knew more.

It was the time when wholesale dealers close
Their shutters with a moody sense of wealth,
But retail dealers, diligent, let loose
The gas (objected to on score of health),
Conveyed in little soldered pipes by stealth,
And make it flare in many a brilliant form,
That all the powers of darkness it repell'th,
Which to the oil-trade doth great scaith and harm,
And supersedeth quite the use of the glow-worm.

Eban, untempted by the pastrycooks,
(Of pastry he got store within the palace,)
With hasty steps, wrapped cloak, and solemn looks,
Incognito upon his errand sallies,
His smelling-bottle ready for the alleys;
He passed the hurdygurdies with disdain,
Vowing he'd have them sent on board the galleys;
Just as he made his vow it 'gan to rain,
Therefore he called a coach, and bade it drive amain.

'I'll pull the string,' said he, and further said,
'Polluted jarvey! Ah, thou filthy hack!
Whose springs of life are all dried up and dead,
Whose linsey-woolsey lining hangs all slack,
Whose rug is straw, whose wholeness is a crack;
And evermore thy steps go clatter-clitter;
Whose glass once up can never be got back,
Who prov'st, with jolting arguments and bitter,
That 'tis of modern use to travel in a litter.

177

'Thou inconvenience! thou hungry crop
For all corn! thou snail-creeper to and fro,
Who, while thou goest, ever seem'st to stop,
And fiddle-faddle standest while you go;
I' the morning, freighted with a weight of woe,
Unto some lazar-house thou journeyest,
And in the evening tak'st a double row
Of dowdies, for some dance or party drest,
Besides the goods meanwhile thou movest east and west.

'By thy ungallant bearing and sad mien,
An inch appears the utmost thou couldst budge;
Yet at the slightest nod, or hint, or sign,
Round to the curb-stone patient dost thou trudge,
Schooled in a beckon, learnèd in a nudge,
A dull-eyed Argus watching for a fare;
Quiet and plodding, thou dost bear no grudge
To whisking tilburies or phaetons rare,
Curricles, or mail-coaches, swift beyond compare.'

Philosophizing thus, he pulled the check
And bade the coachman wheel to such a street,
Who, turning much his body, more his neck,
Louted full low, and hoarsely did him greet:
'Certes, monsieur were best take to his feet,
Seeing his servant can no further drive.
For press of coaches, that to-night here meet,
Many as bees about a straw-capped hive,
When first for April honey into faint flowers they dive.'

Eban then paid his fare, and tiptoe went
To Hum's hotel . . .

LOUIS MacNEICE
(1907–63)

The Taxis

In the first taxi he was alone tra-la,
No extras on the clock. He tipped ninepence
But the cabby, while he thanked him, looked askance
As though to suggest someone had bummed a ride.

In the second taxi he was alone tra-la
But the clock showed sixpence extra; he tipped according
And the cabby from out his muffler said: 'Make sure
You have left nothing behind tra-la between you'.

In the third taxi he was alone tra-la
But the tip-up seats were down and there was an extra
Charge of one-and-sixpence and an odd
Scent that reminded him of a trip to Cannes.

As for the fourth taxi, he was alone
Tra-la when he hailed it but the cabby looked
Through him and said: 'I can't tra-la well take
So many people, not to speak of the dog.'

1961

JAMES BOSWELL
(1740–95)

from *The Life of Dr Johnson*

I again begged his advice as to my method of study at Utrecht. 'Come, (said he) let us make a day of it. Let us go down to Greenwich and dine, and talk of it there.' The following Saturday was fixed for this excursion.

As we walked along the Strand to-night, arm in arm, a woman of the town accosted us, in the usual enticing manner. 'No, no, my girl, (said Johnson) it won't do.' He, however, did not treat her with harshness; and we talked of the wretched life of such women, and agreed, that much more misery than happiness, upon the whole, is produced by illicit commerce between the sexes.

On Saturday, July 30, Dr Johnson and I took a sculler at the Temple-stairs, and set out for Greenwich. I asked him if he really thought a knowledge of the Greek and Latin languages an essential requisite to a good education. JOHNSON. 'Most certainly, Sir, for those who know them have a very great advantage over those who do not. Nay, Sir, it is wonderful what a difference learning makes upon people even in the common intercourse of life, which does not appear to be much connected with it.' 'And yet, (said I) people go through the world very well, and carry on the business of life to good advantage, without learning.' JOHNSON. 'Why, Sir that may be true in cases where learning cannot possibly be of any use; for instance, this boy rows us as well without learning, as if he could sing the song of Orpheus to the Argonauts, who were the first sailors.' He then called to the boy, 'What would you give, my lad, to know about the Argonauts?' 'Sir, (said the boy) I would give what I have.' Johnson was much pleased with his answer, and we gave him a double fare. Dr Johnson then turning to me, 'Sir, (said he) a desire of knowledge is the natural feeling of mankind; and every human being, whose mind is not debauched, will be willing to give all that he has, to get knowledge.'

We landed at the Old Swan, and walked to Billingsgate, where we took oars and moved smoothly along the silver Thames. It was a very fine day. We were entertained with the immense number and variety of ships that were lying at anchor, and with the beautiful country on each side of the river.

★   ★   ★

I was much pleased to find myself with Johnson at Greenwich, which he celebrates in his 'London' as a favourite scene. I had the poem in my pocket, and read the lines aloud with enthusiasm:

> 'On Thames's banks in silent thought we stood,
> Where Greenwich smiles upon the silver flood:
> Pleas'd with the seat which gave ELIZA birth,
> We kneel, and kiss the consecrated earth.'

He remarked that the structure of Greenwich hospital was too magnificent for a place of charity, and that its parts were too much detached, to make one great whole.

Afterwards he entered upon the business of the day, which was to give me his advice as to a course of study. And here I am to mention with much regret, that my record of what he said is miserably scanty. I recollect with admiration an animating blaze of eloquence, which roused every intellectual power in me to the highest pitch, but must have dazzled me so much, that my memory could not preserve the substance of his discourse; for the note which I find of it is no more than this:– 'He ran over the grand scale of human knowledge; advised me to select some particular branch to excel in, but to acquire a little of every kind.' The defect of my minutes will be fully supplied by a long letter upon the subject, which he favoured me with, after I had been some time at Utrecht, and which my readers will have the pleasure to peruse in its proper place.

We walked in the evening in Greenwich Park. He asked me I suppose, by way of trying my disposition, 'Is not this very fine?' Having no exquisite relish of the beauties of Nature, and being more delighted with 'the busy hum of men,' I answered, 'Yes, Sir; but not equal to Fleet-street.' JOHNSON. 'You are right, Sir.'

STUART HENSON
(b. 1954)

Late Train

These carriages have plied their trade all day
in the to-fro heat from King's Cross up to
Peterborough; minute by airless minute
in their net of steel and high wire: the shimmer
on the parallel, throb of the power car –
continuous shrinking to a vanishing-point,
an always-coming, always-getting-there.
And now in the cool night, the vents open
and sucking in the still-warm smells, oily,
unwholesome and evocative, they reel
once more and I leaf through a book, recall
a man in winter clothes waist-deep in grass
who gathered lupins in the wilderness
between the slow-line and the dead canal;
the house-backs and the businesses, the yards;
the curious legend 'May Be Tamped' in rough
block letters on a bridge; and the number
CHAncery 8800, the ghost-phone
of an office-cleaning company, preserved
above graffiti-reach on a warehouse wall.
Now, in the late train, no-one needs to talk,
and at the stops no voice disturbs or shouts
until the sudden bleeping of the doors
announces motion and restores the pulse
that nods these journey-makers on the breast
of sleep and soothes their day-won statuses.
The woman opposite is fair, full-limbed,
and of an age that's done with innocence.
About my age. But still that unselfconscious
rag-doll falling of her head's pure childhood.
Sleep takes us like a mother to her trust.
And as my thought goes straggling at that edge,
I dream of Patsy Toseland and Rosemary,
and Cheryl Dant: the girls who held my hand

on the first day of school in the big land
beyond the garden of my first five years,
or naturally were generous and teased
me with a smile or the promise of a kiss.
The late train rocks these random passengers
till they become all whom I have forgotten
but knew once. Souls journeying by chance,
I muse how you might be asleep somewhere
like this and travelling the spinning night
on other trains to other towns and yet
all drawn down lines of time's discovered map
darkly towards some island of the blessed.

HYLDA SIMS

I Ain't Gauguin Blues
(to be sung to any 12-bar blues sequence)

I'm sittin' on Tahiti drinkin' palm wine and coconut juice
Got the sea got the sun, drinkin' palm wine and coconut juice
Promotion to Papete, an offer I could not refuse

Got this lonesome feelin', feelin' I can't seem to lose
Got this low down lonesome feelin', feelin' I can't seem to lose
Got this cravin' for Belgravia, got the take me back to London
    blues

Don't like these breezes from the ocean, walkin' on the beach
    without my shoes
Can't stand these South Sea breezes, walkin' on the beach without
    my shoes
Got a yen for Big Ben, got the take me back to London blues

I want the grey sky up above me, misery on the South East news
I want the storm clouds gatherin', disaster on the South East news
And I could kill for Piccadilly, got the take me back to London
    blues

I want to breathe in the pollution, stand in the rush hour queues
I want to freak out on the fumes, crush in the rush hour queues
Got a tube train brain, got the take me back to London blues

Don't like this lobster from the ocean, and all this tax free booze
Give me a burger and a Bud, not this fresh sea food and tax free
    booze
I'd try a Wagamama noodle, got the take me back to London blues

I'm stranded on Tahiti drinkin' palm wine and coconut juice
Won't you fly me out of paradise and drop me back in SE22
Don't you know my name ain't Gauguin, got the take me back to
    London blues

CAROLE SATYAMURTI

Heartmarks

This frail-looking balustrade,
all that stood between us and certain
death on the paving-stones below,
is where we frst touched without
a spun glass reticence between us.

That Soho market . . . this revolving door . . .
the layout of the city is peppered
with such places. To fix them
with precise coordinates of words
would arrest their gauzy meanings,

but on the map described by memory
you'll find me whirling nightly
from Bertaux to Pimlico, haunting
Long Acre, Kenwood, Gabriel's Wharf:
all the stations of love.

13

LEAVING

. . . going forward, forward irresistible from Eternity to Eternity.

William Blake, *Jerusalem*

THOMAS DE QUINCEY
(1785–1859)

from *Confessions of an English Opium Eater*

So then, Oxford-street, stony-hearted step-mother! thou that listenest to the sighs of orphans, and drinkest the tears of children, at length I was dismissed from thee: the time was come at last that I no more should pace in anguish thy never-ending terraces; no more should dream, and wake in captivity to the pangs of hunger. Successors, too many, to myself and Ann, have, doubtless, since then trodden in our footsteps – inheritors of our calamities: other orphans than Ann have sighed: tears have been shed by other children: and thou, Oxford-street, hast since, doubtless, echoed to the groans of innumerable hearts. For myself, however, the storm which I had outlived seemed to have been the pledge of a long fair-weather; the premature sufferings which I had paid down, to have been accepted as a ransom for many years to come, as a price for long immunity from sorrow: and if again I walked in London, a solitary and contemplative man (as oftentimes I did), I walked for the most part in serenity and peace of mind. And, although it is true that the calamities of my noviciate in London had struck root so deeply in my bodily constitution that afterwards they shot up and flourished afresh, and grew into a noxious umbrage that has overshadowed and darkened my latter years, yet these second assaults of suffering were met with a fortitude more confirmed, with the resources of a maturer intellect, and with alleviations from sympathising affection – how deep and tender!

LOUIS MacNEICE
(1907–63)

Goodbye to London

Having left the great mean city, I make
Shift to pretend I am finally quit of her
Though that cannot be so long as I work.
   Nevertheless let the petals fall
   Fast from the flower of cities all.

When I first met her to my child's ear
She was an ocean of drums and tumbrils
And in my nostrils horsepiss and petrol.
   Nevertheless let the petals fall
   Fast from the flower of cities all.

Next to my peering teens she was foreign
Names over winking doors, a kaleidoscope
Of wine and ice, of eyes and emeralds.
   Nevertheless let the petals fall
   Fast from the flower of cities all.

Later as a place to live in and love in
I jockeyed her fogs and quoted Johnson:
To be tired of this is to tire of life.
   Nevertheless let the petals fall
   Fast from the flower of cities all.

Then came the headshrinking war, the city
Closed in too, the people were fewer
But closer too, we were back in the womb.
   Nevertheless let the petals fall
   Fast from the flower of cities all.

From which reborn into anticlimax
We endured much litter and apathy hoping
The phoenix would rise, for so they had promised.
   Nevertheless let the petals fall
   Fast from the flower of cities all.

And nobody rose, only some meaningless
Buildings and the people once more were strangers
At home with no one, sibling or friend.
　　Which is why now the petals fall
　　Fast from the flower of cities all.

1962

NOTES ON THE WRITERS
by Anna Adams

Fleur Adcock was born in 1934 at Papakura, New Zealand, but has lived in England since 1963. The poem 'Londoner' is included in her *Poems 1960–2000*, published by Bloodaxe in 2000, and including all her previous collections from Oxford University Press. It was written in the 1970s when the poet was 'rather more in love with London than I am now. I'm still in love with England, though . . .'

Anna Adams was born in London in 1926. 'A Rainbow over Brewer Street' is the first of a sequence of six 'Soho Songs', written in 1986. It was included in *Angels of Soho*, and also in *Nobodies* (Peterloo, 1990). 'Crossing Hungerford Bridge' belongs to 1997, and was printed in the *Rialto*.

Anon is a long-lived and prolific poet, and frequently a woman. He/she has composed love-songs and lullabies, carols, ballads and epics such as the *Kalevala* and *Gilgamesh*. She/he is also responsible for numberless proverbs, myriads of indestructible clichés and immortal jokes, to say nothing of ribald rhymes. As an artist he/she executed the prehistoric cave-murals and the main body of Romanesque and Gothic sculpture. And that is only in Europe. As an inventor, she dreamed up the wheel.

W. H. Auden (1907–73). He grew up in Birmingham and was educated at Gresham's School, Holt, and Christ Church, Oxford. After Oxford he lived in Berlin and was impressed by Bertolt Brecht who, in his turn, had been influenced by Kipling. All through the 1930s Auden's poetry showed his awareness of the growing Nazi tyranny, and his was the most audible voice amongst the other political Thirties' poets. He wrote several plays: *The Dance of Death* (1933); and, with Christopher Isherwood, *The Dog Beneath the Skin* (1935), *The Ascent of F6* (1936), and *On the Frontier* (1938).
This fragment, 'The Londoners' comes from *Plays and Other Dramatic Writings*, edited by Edward Mendelson (Princeton University Press, 1988).

James Berry (b. 1924) was born in Boston, Jamaica, and grew up in Fair Prospect, another coastal village. As a child he 'helped with the growing of crops, the rearing of animals and the general fetching and carrying of food, water – everything.' He spent his late teens working in America, then came to Britain in 1948. At once he knew that he was right for London and England, and England was right for him: 'London had books and accessible libraries. He worked as a telegraphist from 1951 to 1977, and then became a full-time writer. He won the National Poetry Competition with 'Lucy's Letter' in 1981, and has published numerous collections of poetry for both adults and children. He has frequently tutored courses for the Arvon Foundation, and still takes workshops for pupils and teachers in schools, and does many readings abroad for the British Council. He has compiled an anthology of Black poetry in English – *News for Babylon*. Among his collections are *Lucy's Letters and Loving* (1982), *Chain of Days* (Oxford, 1985), and *Hot Earth, Cold Earth* (Bloodaxe, 1995).

William Blake (1757–1827). Something has been said of Blake already in this book, and he has said a great deal for himself. Born near Golden Square, Soho, the self-educated son of a hosier, he was apprenticed to an engraver at the age of fourteen and he would have earned his living by this craft, and prospered, had he not been one of the greatest artist/poets this country has produced. As it was he worked a great deal for no reward because of his surfeit of gifts. He had just enough loyal friends and patrons to keep him going, and at the end of his life a group of admiring young artists – Linnell, Varley, Samuel Palmer, George Richmond and others – gathered round his inspiring presence in his very humble dwelling in Fountain Court. After his death Gilchrist wrote the first biography in 1862, William Rossetti edited some of his poems and published a memoir in 1874; Swinburne admired him; Art Nouveau fed on him; Yeats interpreted him; Geoffrey Keynes edited his complete works; the Beat Poets worshipped him; Kathleen Raine studied him; many biographised him; Enitharmon Perss takes its name from him; the Tate exhibits him and Blake books pour off the presses. There must be at least one www.williamblake.com somewhere on the internet; and the idea of such a non-material dispersed presence might please him.

James Boswell (1740–95), the son of Lord Auchinleck, has been described by Macaulay as 'weak, vain, pushing, curious and garrulous.' He goes on to say that, to Dr Johnson, 'the silly egotism and adulation of Boswell must have been as teasing as the constant buzzing of a fly.' Yet even Macaulay admits that, having gathered material about Johnson for twenty years, Boswell afterwards constructed 'the most interesting biographical work in the world.' This cannot have been entirely owing to its subject.

Boswell had innate journalistic skills and was a born interviewer. On his youthful tour of Europe he interviewed both Rousseau and Voltaire; then, determined to go where no one else went, he visited Corsica and interviewed a famous revolutionary guerrilla leader, and, after his return in 1768 published *An Account of Corsica*. This was successful enough to admit him to the meetings of Goldsmith, Johnson, Garrick, Joshua Reynolds and other leading lights of the day. His most remembered works, though, are the *Journey of a Tour to the Hebrides* (1785) and *The Life of Samuel Johnson* (1791).

Robert Bridges (1844–1930) was educated at Eton and Corpus Christi, Oxford; then he studied medicine at Bart's, practising as a doctor until 1881. At Oxford he met Gerard Manley Hopkins, and they were lifelong friends. Hopkins remained virtually unpublished, but Bridges' first of many books came out in 1873, and he was made Poet Laureate in 1913. In 1916 he published the anthology *Spirit of Man*, containing six poems by Hopkins. This was read by Ivor Gurney, among hundreds of other men in the trenches. *The Testament of Beauty*, a long poem on his spiritual philosophy, came out in 1929, to receive high acclaim and many sales. 'London Snow' is among his best-known lyric poems.

Alan Brownjohn (b. 1931) was born in London and educated at Merton College, Oxford. He taught from 1953 to 1979, before becoming a full-time writer. His first pamphlet of poems was *Travellers Alone* (1954) and his first book, *The Railings* (1961). His *Collected Poems, 1952–1983*, was reissued in 1988 with most of a subsequent collection, *The Old Fleapit*, added on to it. *The Observation Car* followed in 1990. Brownjohn has written for children (*Brownjohn's Beasts*, 1970), edited several anthologies, written a critical study of Philip Larkin, and three novels: *The Way You Tell Them* (1990), *The Long Shadows* (1997) and *A Funny Old Year* (2001). His latest collection is *The Cat Without E-Mail*, from Enitharmon.

Lord Byron (1788–1824) lived with his mother in Aberdeen until he was ten, when he unexpectedly inherited a title and the estate of Newstead Abbey. He was then sent to Harrow School, and at twenty-one took his seat in the House of Lords. After his youthful travels he published *Childe Harold's Pilgrimage*, and 'woke up to find himself famous'. In his short life he was a prolific poet, and his work progressed from the Romantic to the Satiric. His last major work, *Don Juan*, remained unfinished at his death. The first part, published anonymously by John Murray, was denounced as 'filthy and impious' by *Blackwood's Magazine*. The extract from 'Italy versus England' belongs among his later works.

Geoffrey Chaucer (*c.* 1343–1400) was born in London, the son of a vintner. He learned Italian as a boy from the sons of Italian wine-merchants in Lombard Street, and travelled to Italy as a diplomat when he was grown up, for he was a man of action as well as a poet. On his European travels he may have met Boccaccio and Petrarch; certainly he met them through their works. Regarded as the Father of English Literature, he established its character of non-puritanical realism, recording all kinds of men and women with humour, earthiness, compassion and respect. His work has a beautiful freshness. The unfinished 'Cook's Tale' comes from Chaucer's most famous work, *The Canterbury Tales*.

John Clare (1793–1864) was born in Helpston, Northamptonshire, the son of a farm-labourer. After a minimal education he began to write poetry in his early teens, and he had enough success to dream that he might live by his pen. He had seven children by his wife Patty, and, though he had some patronage, it was not enough, and he had to spend much time on fieldwork. But, as he said, he found his poems in the fields. It could be considered wonderful that he stayed sane as long as he did, but in 1837 he began his career as madman as well as poet. He was confined at first at High Beach, in Essex, and then from 1841 until the end of his life in Northampton, where he was humanely treated and granted much freedom. Like his verse, his prose is entirely unpunctuated, though full of more essential literary skills. The extracts in this book are from the journals that Clare kept on his three journeys to London.

Amy Clampitt (1920–92) was a New Yorker born of a prairie-settler family. As well as wide reading and an informed interest in art, she had knowledge of botany and geology, and both sciences enriched her vocabulary and imagery. Her first book, *The Kingfisher*, appeared to considerable acclaim when she was fifty-three. Its title was a tribute to Gerard Manley Hopkins. Another hero was Keats; her worship is visible in such phrases as 'the very tissue of desire'. The Wordsworths, Coleridge, George Eliot, Virginia Woolf, Simone Weil, ancient history and myths all animate her poems. She was an American more than half in love with Europe, and she fed on art and literature quite as much as on life, or nature.

The Kingfisher was succeeded by *What the Light Was Like*, and, in 1987, *Archaic Figure*.

Arthur Hugh Clough (1819–61). The son of a cotton merchant, he was educated at Rugby and Balliol College, Oxford. His best-known poems – 'Say not the Struggle naught Availeth', 'There is no God', the satirical 'Latest Decalogue', and 'How Pleasant it is to have Money', deal with the struggle between faith and doubt, his perception of the humbug in much religious practise, and the social injustice of 'Christian' societies.

David Constantine (b. 1944) was born in Salford, Lancashire. He read Modern Languages at Wadham College, Oxford, and is now a Fellow of Queen's College, Oxford. His first book of poems was *A Brightness to Cast Shadows* (Bloodaxe, 1980), followed by *Watching for Dolphins* and *Madder*. 'The Forest' is included among the new work in his *Selected Poems*, published in 1991. Constantine has also published a novel, *Davies*, and a long poem *Caspar Hauser*, about the enigmatic boy of Nuremburg. His translation of a selection of poems by Hölderlin won the 1997 European Poetry Translation prize, and he has more recently translated Hölderlin's *Translations of Sophocles*. Constantine's latest collection of his own poems, *Something for the Ghosts*, was published in 2002.

John Davidson (1857–1909) worked for twenty-seven years as a schoolmaster in Scotland before he settled in London in 1899, to live by his pen. He contributed to *The Yellow Book* and in 1893 published his *Fleet Street Eclogues*. The first two parts of *The Theatrocrat God and Mammon* came out in 1907. 'Thirty Bob a Week' is Davidson's best known ballad.

Thomas De Quincey (1785–1859) was born in Manchester and educated in Bath and at Manchester Grammar School, from which he ran away and so endured the homelessness he describes in his most famous book, *Confessions of an English Opium Eater* (1822). After his down-and-out period he studied at Oxford, where his laudanum habit began, and though he managed to get through life, supporting his family by freelance writing, he never fully recovered from his addiction, so his early masterpiece remains his most coherent work. Nevertheless, his imagination and originality influenced many other writers – most obviously Poe and Baudelaire.

Charles Dickens (1812–70) was born at Portsmouth, the son of a naval clerk. After moving to Chatham, the improvident father was imprisoned for debt when the boy Dickens was twelve, so he was sent out to work in a blacking warehouse where he acquired his magnificent anger on behalf of neglected, uneducated and overworked children. He made a reputation reporting parliamentary debates for the *Morning Chronicle* and contributed 'Sketches by Boz' to the *Monthly Magazine*. *The Pickwick Papers* became a great success in 1837 and in the same year Dickens married Catherine Hogarth. *Bleak House*, from which these extracts are taken, was written in 1852 and 1853.

Thomas Stearns Eliot (1888–1965) was born in Missouri and educated at Harvard, the Sorbonne and Merton College, Oxford. In London he worked in Lloyd's Bank, and in 1927 took British citizenship and became a member of the Anglican Church. He had published *Prufrock and Other Observations* in 1917, founded *The Criterion* in 1922, and published *The Waste Land* in it. In 1922 he left the bank and joined Faber and Faber where he built up a formidable list of poets: Pound, Auden, MacNeice, Spender, David Jones, etc.

D. J. Enright (b. 1920) was born in Leamington and educated in Cambridge. For many years he taught English Literature in the Far East, which explains the settings and themes of some of his poems. His first collection was *Laughing Hyena and Other Poems* (1953), to be followed by many others. He has published a novel, books of critical essays, including *Man Is an Onion*, and an autobiographical memoir called *Memoirs of a Mendicant Professor*. 'The Stations of King's Cross', originally in *Sad Ires* of 1975, is included in his *Collected Poems, 1948–1998*.

U. A. Fanthorpe (b. 1929). Born in Kent, she was educated in Surrey and Oxford, then taught for sixteen years. She then abandoned a respectable salary for a job as a hospital clerk in Bristol, and this experience pitchforked her into poetry. Her first collection, *Side Effects*, was published in 1978 by Peterloo Poets, and the same publisher subsequently brought out *Standing To* (1982); *Voices Off* (1984); *A Watching Brief* (1987); *Neck-Verse* (1992); *Safe as Houses* (1995), and *Consequences*. The last four have all been Poetry Book Society Recommendations. Her King Penguin *Selected Poems* came out in 1986, and her work is in *Penguin Modern Poets 6*.

The poet says that 'Counting Song' was suggested by frequent crossings of Hungerford Bridge from Charing Cross to the South Bank. 'There always seemed to be Cardboard Citizens camping out there, with dogs and babies.'

'Underground' is about the surreal wartime Underground when the platforms and passageways were also dormitories, and we waited for trains while people camped at our feet, reading to their children, eating snack suppers, or sleeping undisturbed as people and noisy trains arrived and departed. U. A. Fanthorpe sees it through the medium of sculptor Henry Moore's historic *Shelter Sketchbook*, first published in 1945.

John Greening (b. 1954). He grew up in London, close to the Thames. Since *Nightflights*, his New and Selected Poems were published by Rockingham Press, his song-cycle, *Falls*, with music by Paul Mottram, has been performed at the Wigmore Hall. A long poem, *Omm Sety*, appeared from the Shoestring Press in 2001, and he has been awarded a grant by the Society of Authors to travel in Iceland. 'Kew' has been published in *Critical Survey*.

Thomas Hardy (1840–1928). The son of a stonemason, Hardy left school at sixteen, to be apprenticed to an architect in London. He was not able to replace this first profession with full-time writing before he had written several novels and had a great success with *Far from the Madding Crowd* in 1874. By this time he was married and living again in his native Dorset, the 'Wessex' of most of his fiction and the setting of many poems. All through his life he wrote poetry as well as prose, and after sixty years his poems numbered more than 900. Thomas Hardy had much influence on twentieth-century poets who appreciated his stoic agnosticism, his realism, and his understanding of country matters.

'A Thunderstorm in Town' and 'Beyond the Last Lamp' come from the Lyrics and Reveries in *Satires of Circumstance*, 'The Coronation' from *Miscellaneous Pieces*, and 'A Refusal' from *Winter Words*, all in the *Collected Poems of Thomas Hardy*, published by Macmillan in 1952.

James Harpur (b. 1956). A resident of Hammersmith and Chiswick for many years, he now lives in Devon. He has had three books published by Anvil Press, *A Vision of Comets* (1993), *The Monk's Dream* (1996) and the most recent *Oracle Bones*

(2001). He has received awards from the Eric Gregory Trust, the Arts Council and The Society of Authors. In 2001 he was poet in residence at Exeter Cathedral as part of the National Year of the Artist scheme.

'My Father's Flat', which is published in *The Monk's Dream*, is part of a seven-sonnet sequence called 'The Frame of Furnace Light' that won the 1995 National Poetry Competition.

John Heath-Stubbs (b. 1918) was educated at Worcester College for the Blind and Queen's College, Oxford. He was first published in *Eight Oxford Poets* in 1941. Numerous and varied collections followed. He describes himself as a traditionalist, and sees tradition as continual change. He is learned in the Classics, in natural history and in European poetry and arts. His *A Charm Against the Toothache* (1954) contains poems of modern London, but 'The Philosophers and the Pomes' and 'London Magpie' are from *Sweetapple Earth* (1993). In the same year he published an autobiography, *Hindsights*.

Stuart Henson (b. 1954) won an Eric Gregory Award in 1979. 'Late Train' is from *Ember Music*, published by Peterloo Poets in 1994. His most recent publication is *Clair de Lune* from Shoestring Press in 1998. 'Late Train' was written after an excursion to hear Anthony Hecht read at the South Bank: 'All the details are genuine.'

Thomas Hood (1799–1845) was born in London, the son of a bookseller. He was a prolific writer of light verse, a friend of Hazlitt, Lamb and De Quincey, and he edited several magazines. One of his most successful and remembered serious poems is 'The Song of the Shirt', about the sweated labour of seamstresses. Other much anthologised poems are 'I remember, I remember' and this one – 'November'.

Frances Horovitz (1938–83). Born in London as Frances Hooker, she read English and Drama at Bristol University, then studied at RADA. She worked as an actress and broadcaster, frequently reading poetry for the BBC. Her collections include *The High Tower, Water over Stone*, and *Snow Light, Water Light*. She was often concerned with landscape, firstly of Gloucestershire and latterly of Northumberland where she lived for a few years before her early death. Her *Collected Poems* were jointly published by Bloodaxe and Enitharmon.

Ted Hughes (1930–98). Born in West Yorkshire, the son of a carpenter who had survived the trenches of the First World War, Hughes was educated at Mexborough Grammar School and Pembroke College Cambridge, where he first read English, before changing to Anthropology. In some ways his boyhood resembled that of Wordsworth, for he was able to run wild in wild country. His elder brother was a gamekeeper, and with him he went fishing and shooting, and learned animal and bird lore. Such knowledge played a major part in the imagery of his early poems. His first book was *A Hawk in the Rain* (1957), then came *Lupercal* (1960) and *Wodwo* (1967). *Crow* (1970) turned a corner in his writing, for his previous animals had been, in the main, real animals, but his Crow is a mythological bird of death and decomposition. *Cave Birds* followed in 1975, but with the lyrical *Season Songs* (1976) he is back in a natural nature, as he is in *Moortown* (1979). These books reflect the happiness of his second marriage, as well as his sorrow for his Devon farmer father-in-law.

Hughes also wrote poems and stories for children. He was made Poet Laureate in 1984, and he finished his writing career triumphantly with his free translations of *Tales from Ovid* and the sequence of *Birthday Letters* – 88 poems describing his relationship with his first wife, the poet Sylvia Plath. The poem included here is from that book, and refers back to the period when Hughes and Plath were living in North London.

Dr Samuel Johnson (1709–84) is better remembered now for his Dictionary, and for the utterances recorded by James Boswell, than as a poet: yet it was his poem 'London', published when the writer was twenty-eight, that first drew attention to him from the literary world of eighteenth-century London.

Born the son of a Lichfield bookseller who was intelligent and pious but not businesslike, Johnson had much first-hand experience of poverty. After leaving school at sixteen he spent two years at home reading his father's stock. Then a neighbour volunteered to support him through three years at Pembroke College, Oxford, but the payments failed, so that Samuel the student was seen as a comically clumsy and ragged figure with holes in his shoes. He was also proud and rebellious, and refused charity, so – though a brilliant scholar – he had to leave prematurely, without a degree. At home again, the young Johnson supported himself by literary drudgery and jobs as a school usher. When he was twenty-six he married Elizabeth Porter, a widow many years his senior. They moved to London in 1737.

While establishing his reputation as a poet, essayist and lexicographer, Johnson faced prolonged periods of poverty until with the publication of his *Dictionary* (1755) and *Rasselas* (1759) his reputation was secure, and in 1762 he was awarded a pension by George III of £300 a year. In 1763 the young James Boswell entered his life and systematically recorded Dr Johnson's discourse, and, in 1773, they travelled together to the Hebrides. This resulted in two books, Johnson's appearing as *A Journey to the Western Islands of Scotland* (1775), while Boswell's *Journal of a Tour to the Hebrides* came out ten years later, after Johnson's death. Samuel Johnson's later years had been made happier by his sixteen-year friendship with Mr and Mrs Thrale, a prosperous brewer and his witty young wife who always made him welcome. Johnson's last extended work was *The Lives of the English Poets* (1779–81). He died at his house in Bolt Court, off Fleet Street, on 13 December 1784, leaving his estate to his black servant.

John Keats (1795–1821). In spite of his short life, John Keats was one of the principal poets of the English Romantic movement, which began with Thomas Chatterton, who had the shortest life of all (1752–70), and to whom Keats dedicated his ambitious early poem *Endymion*. Keats's 'annus mirabilis' lasted from the autumn of 1818 until autumn 1819, when he wrote 'The Eve of St Agnes', 'The Eve of St Mark', the great Odes, including this one to the Nightingale, 'Lamia' and several other poems. When he was already ill with the disease that killed him, he began 'The Cap and Bells', a satire set in a 'Fairyland' that is really London. As well as poetry, Keats wrote a series of brilliant and penetratingly wise letters – to his brothers, to his young sister Fanny, to his friends and publishers, and the girl he loved, Fanny Brawne.

Rudyard Kipling (1865–1936). Born in Bombay and educated in England, where his childhood was far from happy. He returned to India when he was seventeen and worked as a journalist and editor on newspapers in Lahore and Allahabad. After this apprenticeship, on his return to England he was at once successful. He was a very prolific writer of poems, stories, articles, novels and children's books, and, because he could be, at times, a voice for the common soldier, and the common civilian too, and because his highly skilled verses spoke from the heart, he was popularly regarded as the unofficial Poet Laureate. He never became the official one. In 1907 he was the first English writer to receive the Nobel Prize for Literature.

'London Stone' expresses some of the ongoing grief that almost every individual must have suffered, to some degree, after the carnage of the First World War.

Charles Lamb (1775–1834) was born in London, the youngest child of a lawyer's clerk. From the age of seven to fourteen he was educated at Christ's Hospital school (like Coleridge), and his wish was to enter holy orders, but his stammer disqualified him from preaching, and lack of funds at home forbade further studies. So he went to work, firstly at South Sea House and then, at seventeen, to East India House where he remained until he was fifty. In 1796 he suffered a brief period of insanity, which his gift for writing may have helped to cure; but, later in the same year, his sister Mary suffered a much more serious bout of madness, and killed her bedridden mother and injured their childish old father. These events caused Charles to renounce any thoughts of marriage, and, as soon as his father had died, he took upon himself the care of his sister. He had the rock-solid sense of responsibility that his friend Coleridge lacked, and neither in his life nor his art did he kick over the traces. Lamb wrote numerous highly individual essays, a handful of poems, and – with his sister – *Tales from Shakespeare*, *Mrs Leicester's School*, and *The Adventures of Ulysses*, all aimed at children.

The extracts included come from Lamb's two collections of *Essays of Elia*, published in 1823 and 1833.

Louis MacNeice (1907–63) was born in Ulster, the son of a Prostestant clergyman, and was educated at Marlborough and Oxford. He taught in Birmingham and then became a resident Londoner who wrote about his city frequently. It would have been possible to use many passages from his *Autumn Journal* of 1938, which was written during the Munich crisis, but I prefer to recommend it, as a wonderfully enjoyable long poem, and to use short lyrics instead. There are two poems from the war years about the air-raids and London burning. I was unable to resist his 'Farewell to London' as it makes a fitting end, and MacNeice's refrain carries us back to the beginning of the *Thames* anthology (Enitharmon Press, 1999) and Dunbar's refrain, proving that enjoyment of modern poetry is enhanced by knowledge of the living words of the dead.

Glyn Maxwell (b. 1962) was born in Welwyn Garden City, the son of a scientist and an actress. Educated at Oxford, he subsequently won a scholarship in poetry and playwriting at Boston University, USA, and in 1990 his first collection of poetry, *Tale of the Mayor's Son* came out, to much acclaim, from Bloodaxe. 'The Fires of the River' was included in his second collection, *Out of the Rain*, published by Bloodaxe in 1992.

Felix Mendelssohn (1809–47), the German composer, wrote brilliant letters home while on his many professional visits abroad.

Grace Nichols (b. 1950) was born at Stanleyville in Guyana, and had begun to work as a journalist before moving to London in 1977. In 1983 her first book of poems, *I Is a Long Memoried Woman*, established her as a poet blending Creole and Standard English. Since then *The Fat Black Woman's Poems* (1984), *Lazy Thoughts of a Lazy Woman* (1989) and *Sunris* have consolidated her reputation. She has also written a novel, *Whole of a Morning Sky* (1986), and is a prolific writer for children.

William Oxley (b. 1939) was born in Manchester and has devoted his life to poetry, criticism, playwriting and editing. Widely published, his most recent books are his autobiography *No Accounting for Paradise* from Rockingham Press in 1999, and his *New and Selected Poems*, from the same publisher, in 2001. 'The Bitter Cry of Outcast London' is one of an as yet unpublished series of poems called 'London Visions'.

Peter Phillips (b. 1948). Born in London, where he still lives. He has published a pamphlet, *Frayed at the Edges* (Hearing Eye Press, 1997), and a first full collection, *Looking for You* (2001), from the same publisher.

Ruth Pitter (1897–1992) was born in Ilford, East London, where her parents were schoolteachers. She was well known as a poet in her lifetime; in 1955 she was the first woman to receive the Queen's Gold Medal for Poetry, and she was made a C.B.E. in 1979. Her work is very various – both emotional and moving, sometimes metaphysical, but it can also be rumbustiously humorous. She tells significant stories, and had a considerable knowledge of natural history, which she made good use of in her poetry. She was also a brilliant writer of comic verse. 'Musa Translated' is the first half of a Second World War poem. The succeeding 46 lines are set in the country. The poem was in *Pitter on Cats* (1947), and that whole book is included in her *Collected Poems*, published by Enitharmon Press in 1996, with an introduction by Elizabeth Jennings.

Kathleen Raine (b. 1908). Born of a Scottish mother and a Northumbrian schoolmaster father, she was educated at Girton College, Cambridge, where she read biology. Her first book of poems was *Stone and Flower*, published in 1943 by Tambimuttu's Editions Poetry London. She has published three volumes of autobiographical prose: *Farewell Happy Fields* (1973), *The Land Unknown* (1975), and *The Lion's Mouth* (1977), as well as several other books of verse, culminating in her *Collected Poems* of 2000 (Golgonooza Press). One of her major achievements is her study of William Blake which seeks out Blake's intellectual forebears and the ancestors of his new-made mythological figures. She also founded the Temenos Academy in 1981. It is devoted to spiritual art, and academic papers on the mystical religions, many of them published in the journal *Temenos* and its successor, the *Temenos Academy Review*.

Carole Satyamurti lives in London and earns her living as a sociologist, teaching at the University of East London and the Tavistock Clinic. She won the National Poetry Competition in 1986, and received a Cholmondeley Award in 2000. Her *Broken Moon* (OUP, 1987) and *Striking Distance* (OUP, 1994) were Poetry Book Society Recommendations. 'Love and Variations' (2000), as well as her *Selected Poems*, are available from Bloodaxe.

Percy Bysshe Shelley (1792–1822) was educated at Eton and University College Oxford. This education did not bring about a conventional result, however, and his intellectual rebellion at Oxford culminated in his pamphlet *The Necessity of Atheism*, for which he was sent down. At nineteen he eloped with Harriet Westbrook, and Shelley married her, against his principles and his father's wishes, in August 1811. The marriage lasted three years, while Harriet produced two children and Shelley wrote pamphlets on vegetarianism, a Declaration of Rights, and the poem of ideas, *Queen Mab*. He was always as much concerned with social reform as poetry, though he could (and did) write purely beautiful (though not meaningless) lyrics. When Shelley made the acquaintance of Mary Godwin – the daughter of Mary Wollstonecraft – his marriage with Harriet was doomed. Shelley eloped again, abroad this time, and the new couple took Mary's stepsister, Claire Clairmont, along with them.

The Shelley story is as strewn with corpses as a Jacobean stage. Harriet drowned herself in the Serpentine, and Fanny too committed suicide. Both Harriet's children died in foster-care, and only one of Shelley's three children by Mary survived. A year after the death of young Keats at Rome, which gave rise to Shelley's poem *Adonais*, Shelley, aged twenty-nine, was drowned in the bay of Lerici.

Peter Bell the Third was written during Shelley's most productive year (1819–20) when in spite of grief he also finished *Prometheus*, wrote *The Mask of Anarchy*, 'Ode to the West Wind' and his political odes – 'To Liberty' and 'To Naples'; also the verse-letter to Maria Gisborne; 'The Witch of Atlas' and several shorter poems: the famous 'To a Skylark' and 'The Cloud' among them; and he wrote a play, *The Cenci*.

Jon Silkin (1930–97) was born in London and educated at Wycliffe and Dulwich Colleges. He established himself as a poet while working as a manual labourer, a few years after the Second World War. His first book of poems, *The Peaceable Kingdom* (1954) was published shortly after he had founded the literary magazine *Stand*. The poet could still be seen, as late as the 1980s, when he was well known and the magazine had an international circulation, selling the latest issue in the street outside the Public Library in Newcastle-upon-Tyne.

Hylda Sims has lived in London since the 1950s. She writes poetry, songs and novels and has worked as a folksinger and as a teacher. Her published writing includes *Reaching Peckham* – a narrative sequence of poems based on Peckham in South London (Left Bank Press, 1996) – and a novel, *Inspecting the Island* (Seven-ply Yarns, 2001) based on A. S. Neill's self-government school, Summerhill, where she was a pupil. Her poetry has also appeared in anthologies and magazines. Currently, she co-runs Poetry & Jazz at London's Poetry Café in Covent Garden.

Stevie Smith (1902–71) was born in Hull and baptised Florence Margaret, which names were soon superseded. On the desertion of her father, Stevie and her sister, mother and aunt moved south, to Palmers Green in North London. There both girls grew up, and Stevie remained in the same house, in Avondale Road, all her life. There she wrote three novels and innumerable poems of a subtle quiddity. They can be amusing, sad, religious or angry – simultaneously. 'The Birds of Avondale' celebrates her suburb, and 'A Soldier dear to Us' describes the brave gaity of wasted young men, and gives us a clue to Stevie's development as a poet.

Sir Stephen Spender (1909–95) grew up in Hampstead, London. While a student at Oxford he met the impressively promising young writers W. H. Auden, Louis MacNeice and Christopher Isherwood. His first collection, *Twenty Poems*, came out in 1930, and was closely followed by *Poems* (1933) which included a poem called 'Pylons' and others full of the new imagery that characterised the Thirties Poets, and caused them, for a while, to be called 'Pylon Poets'. During the Second World War Spender was a member of the Fire Service, and no doubt his active intimacy with the air-raids gave rise to this poem.

Anne Stevenson (b. 1933) was born in England of American parents. She was educated in the U.S.A. but has spent most of her adult life in England. She is the author of numerous books of poetry, critical prose, and a biography of Sylvia Plath. 'All Canal Boat Cruises Start Here' was written in the early 1980s when her daughter Caroline was expecting her first baby. Caroline had been born in post-war London in the mid 1950s, and Anne, herself back in London, wrote the poem 'to express that curious sense of continuity through time that London always produces in me, no matter how much its surfaces change.' Stevenson's latest collection, *Granny Scarecrow*, was published by Bloodaxe Books in 2001, and *Poems, 1955–1995* is still in print, also from Bloodaxe.

Jonathan Swift (1667–1745) is most famous for having written *Gulliver's Travels*, but he wrote many other things besides, in both poetry and prose. Born in Dublin, he was educated at Trinity College, Dublin, and ordained in 1694 at Kilroot. His *The Battle of the Books* and *A Tale of a Tub* were popular successes when they were published in 1704. His *Journal to Stella* describes his life in London to Stella – who may have been his wife – living in Dublin. Much of Swift's work was satirical, fired by anger at abuses. *A Modest Proposal*, motivated by compassion for the condition of Ireland's poor, is one of his best-known satires. In it he suggests that the babies of the poor should be fattened to feed the rich. It would be 'innocent, cheap, easy, effectual,' he says, and a logical conclusion to the callousness that already prevailed. Swift spent the last thirty years of his life in Dublin, where he was much loved, and famous for charitable works.

Vernon Watkins (1906–67) was born in Wales and educated at Magdalene College, Cambridge. He lived near Swansea, and worked as a bank-clerk and teacher. Watkins' first collection of verse, *The Ballad of the Mari Lwyd*, was published in 1941, to be followed by many others – *The Lamp and the Veil* (1945), *Cypress and Acacia* (1959), *Fidelities* (1968) and *Selected Poems, 1930–1960*.

Virginia Woolf (1882–1941) was born in London, the daughter of Sir Leslie and Lady Stephen. On the death of their father, Virginia, Vanessa (the painter) and their brothers moved to Bloomsbury, and in the course of time became the core of the Bloomsbury Group. Virginia married Leonard Woolf in 1912 and her first novel, *The Voyage Out*, was published in 1915. The Woolfs founded the Hogarth Press together in 1917. Her works include *Jacob's Room* (1922), *Mrs Dalloway* (1925), *To the Lighthouse* (1927), *Orlando* (1928), *The Waves* (1931), *Flush* (1933), *The Years* (1937), and *Between the Acts*, published posthumously in 1941 after Woolf's suicide.

William Wordsworth (1770–1850) was born at Cockermouth, Cumbria, and educated at Hawkshead Grammar School and St John's College, Cambridge. As a 'Lake Poet' he is not thought of as having had much to do with London, though he visited occasionally, and he figures in Keats's letters in early 1818. As a young man Wordsworth had lived in London from January to September 1795, after his return from France. City life did not suit him, though he enjoyed the theatre and the 'grave Follies' of courts, parliaments and church services. The extracts from *The Prelude* are from the revised version, published posthumously in 1850.

Kit Wright (b. 1944). Born in Kent and educated at Cambridge, he is well known as a writer for both adults and children, and as an editor, wit and broadcaster. 'The Fortunes of War' is included in his *Poems 1974–1983*, published by Hutchinson in 1988. No doubt it is also in *Hoping it Might be So*, new and selected poems, brought out by Leviathan in 2000.

Benjamin Zephaniah (b. 1958). Though born in Birmingham, he spent a large part of his childhood in Jamaica. As a teenager in Handsworth he was sent to an approved school for being rebellious and he was even sent to prison for burglary. But he turned to music and poetry and emerged as a performance poet with the anti-racist demonstrations of the late 1970s and early '80s. He has given readings all over the world, has published two poetry collections for children and two for adults, and he also writes moving plays. 'Neighbours' and 'City River Blues' are from *Propa Propaganda* (Bloodaxe, 1996).

ACKNOWLEDGEMENTS

Acknowledgements for helpful suggestions and encouragement are due to John Greening, Roger Scott, John Rowe (met as a stranger at a Troubadour Coffee House reading – he recommended Charles Lamb's essays), Graham Fawcett (whose lectures have recently broadened my horizons), the staff of The Poetry Library (for bibliographical guidance), Tom Durham, Stephen Stuart-Smith and Chloë Greenwood. I would like to dedicate this book to the memory of my father, George Butt, who was a born-and-bred Londoner who loved poetry.

Anna Adams

★

Enitharmon Press gratefully acknowledges permission to reprint the following:

FLEUR ADCOCK: 'Londoner' from *Poems 1960-2000* (Bloodaxe, 2000), by permission of the author; W. H. AUDEN: 'The Londoners' from *Plays and Other Dramatic Writings*, ed. Edward Mendelson (Faber and Faber, 1988), by permission of the editor and publishers; JAMES BERRY: 'Lucy's Letter' from *Lucy's Letters and Loving* (New Beacon, 1982) and 'The Coming of Yams and Mangoes and Mountain Honey' from *Hinterland: Caribbean Poetry from the West Indies and Britain*, ed. E.A. Markham (Bloodaxe, 1989), by permission of the author; ALAN BROWNJOHN: 'The Cities' from *The Cat Without E-Mail* (Enitharmon Press, 2001), by permission of the author; AMY CLAMPITT: 'London, Inside and Outside' from *Collected Poems* (Faber and Faber, 1998), by permission of the publishers; DAVID CONSTANTINE: 'The Forest' from *Selected Poems* (Bloodaxe, 1991), by permission of the author; T. S. ELIOT: Extract from 'The Waste Land' from *Collected Poems 1909-1962* (Faber and Faber, 1963), by permission of the publishers; D. J. ENRIGHT: 'The Stations of King's Cross' from *Collected Poems 1948-1998* (OUP/Carcanet Press, 1998), by permission of the author; U. A. FANTHORPE: 'Counting Song' from *Safe as Houses* (Peterloo Poets, 1995) and 'Underground', by permission of the author; JOHN GREENING: 'At Tate Modern' and 'Kew', by permission of the author; JAMES HARPUR: 'My Father's Flat' from *The Monk's Dream* (Anvil Press, 1996), by permission of the author; JOHN HEATH-STUBBS: 'London Magpie' and 'The Philosophers and the Pomes' from *Sweetapple Earth* (Carcanet Press, 1993), by permission of the author; STUART HENSON: 'Late Train' from *Ember Music* (Peterloo Poets, 1994), by permission of the author; FRANCES HOROVITZ: 'Romeo and Juliet at the Old Vic' from *Collected Poems* (Bloodaxe/Enitharmon Press, 1985), by permission of Roger Garfitt; TED HUGHES: 'Epiphany' from *Birthday Letters* (Faber and Faber, 1998), by permission of the Estate of Ted Hughes, and the publishers; RUDYARD KIPLING: 'London Stone', by permission of A. P. Watt Ltd on behalf of The National Trust for Places of Historical Interest or Natural Beauty; LOUIS MacNEICE: 'Goodbye to London', 'The Taxis' and 'Troll's Courtship' from *Collected Poems* (Faber and Faber, 1966), by permission of David Higham Associates; GLYN MAXWELL: 'The Fires by the River' from *Out of the Rain* (Bloodaxe, 1992), by permission of the publishers; GRACE NICHOLS: 'Island